Getting Organized

"I can guarantee you one thing, Sid...it's here in our infallible files, neatly nestled somewhere between A and Z."

Getting Organized

The easy way to put your life in order

STEPHANIE WINSTON

 WARNER BOOKS

A Warner Communications Company

WARNER BOOKS EDITION

Copyright © 1978 by Stephanie Winston

ALL RIGHTS RESERVED

This Warner Books Edition is published by arrangement
with W.W. Norton & Company

Cover design by Bob Antler
Illustrations by Susanne Strohbach
Frontispiece cartoon by Saxon, courtesy of Oxford Pendaflex
Corporation

Warner Books, Inc., 666 Fifth Avenue, New York, N.Y. 10103

Ⓦ A Warner Communications Company

Printed in the United States of America
First Printing: October 1979
10 9 8

Library of Congress Cataloging in Publication Data

Winston, Stephanie.
   Getting organized.

   Reprint of the 1978 ed. published by Norton, New York.
   Bibliography: p. 243
   Includes index.
   1. Home economics.   2. Time allocation.   I. Title.
[TX147.W75 1979]   640   79-10485
ISBN 0-446-37956-5 (U.S.A.)
ISBN 0-446-37957-3 (Canada)

Contents

Contents

Contents

Preface

This book answers two different kinds of questions about being organized. The first is the nuts-and-bolts "how-to": how do I take control of paperwork, arrange a hectic schedule, organize my books, clear out the closets? What are some innovative ideas for getting the most from available space? For these purposes, *Getting Organized* is a straightforward reference, similar to a dictionary or encyclopedia. Consult the table of contents or extensive index for the pages that deal with your problem and work from there.

The second question, more personal and more pervasive in its effect, is, "How can I clarify the confusions of my life?" *Getting Organized* clarifies the reasons why many people feel that things are out of control, the basic attitudes involved and, most important, new ways to think about time and physical environment to give life a coherent shape.

Whichever approach speaks most strongly to you, I recommend that you read through the entire book before turning to specific organizing tasks, because familiarity with the basics of good organizing is so important.

The background I draw upon is primarily my own experience as director of the firm The Organizing Principle. We work in offices designing paperwork flow, filing systems, time management, staff deployment, and physical layout; and in homes, working with personal paperwork, kitchens, closets, and general household functions. Such a wide range of experience has made it possible for me to pin-point the specific areas in which systems design has a place, and to recognize the basic attitudes that foster good organizing in any situation.

I would be glad to know of any planning or organizing tips from your own experience, or any suggestions on the book you may care to offer. Please write to me c/o W. W. Norton & Company Inc., 500 Fifth Avenue, New York, N.Y. 10036. All correspondence will be received with interest and appreciation.

Organizing is fun, really—once you get the knack it becomes almost a game. Approach the task with a light spirit; there is hardly anything more satisfying than clearing things up around you. So good luck, and enjoy it!

STEPHANIE WINSTON

New York City
May 1978

Acknowledgments

I would like to thank the people whose confidence and encouragement was so important to me in establishing my business and writing this book: my parents, Miriam and Harry Winston; my sisters, Terry Winston and Dinah Lovitch; and Ruth Stark, Margaret and Sheldon Klein, Shirley and Lou Winston, Marnie Winston Feinberg, and Joshua Winston.

Norma Fox, the best of friends, offered me the use of her offices at Human Sciences Press (thanks also to Dr. Sheldon Roen), where I wrote much of this book. Emily Fox Kales was always *there*. Ann Jackowitz was a loyal and steadfast friend, and Sanford Schmidt too.

Specific ideas used in the book were contributed by: Dinah Lovitch, gourmet cook *extraordinaire*, who helped me with the kitchen chapter; Faith MacFadden and close friends Sara Miles and Muriel Gelbart, who defined the conundrums of children and family life; and students Chris Clark, Don Goalstone, Joan Masket, Marjorie Atwood Murray, and Julius Shulman.

The organizing of *Getting Organized* was accomplished by Susan Ann Protter, literary agent and friend, and the *three* fine editors it was my privilege to work with: Carol Houck Smith, Sharon Morgan, and Chris Steinmetz. Thank you all.

S. W.

How Organized Are You?

1. Does it often take you more than ten minutes to unearth a particular letter, bill, report or other paper from your files (or piles of paper on your desk)?

2. Are there papers on your desk, other than reference materials, that you haven't looked through for a week or more?

3. Has your electricity or another utility ever been turned off because you forgot to pay the bill?

4. Within the last two months, have you forgotten any scheduled appointment, anniversary, or specific date you wanted to acknowledge?

5. Do magazines and newspapers pile up unread?

6. Do you frequently procrastinate so long on a work assignment that it becomes an emergency or panic situation?

7. Has anything ever been misplaced in your home or office for longer than two months?

8. Do you often misplace doorkeys, glasses, gloves, handbag, briefcase, or other "regulars"?

9. Is your definition of "organized space" to fit as many objects as you can into a limited area?

10. Do things amass in corners of closets, or on the floor, because you can't decide where to put them?

11. Do you feel that your storage problems would be solved if you had more space?

12. Do you want to get organized, but everything is in such a mess that you don't know where to start?

13. Do your children have clear-cut household assignments that they carry out willingly?

14. By the end of an average day, have you accomplished at least the most important tasks you set for yourself?

15. Do you regularly take advantage of housecleaning help, babysitters, dry cleaners, other services? (Assuming money isn't a serious impediment.)

16. Are the kitchen items you use most often in the most convenient place?

17. Is your living room arranged so that family and/or guests can speak comfortably without raising their voices? are there places for drinks and snacks?

SCORING: Questions 1–12 one point for each "yes"
Questions 13–17 one point for each "no"

IF YOUR SCORE IS:

1–4 Systems are under control. Some of the innovative tips in this book might make things even better.

5–8 Disorganization is troublesome. The book's program could help considerably.

9–11 Life must be very difficult. Careful study and execution of the program outlined in the book is advisable.

12 Disorganized to the point of chaos. Following
AND UP the book's program could change your life.

PART ONE

The Organizing Principle

1
On Getting It All Together

More than once you may have felt that someone wasn't looking when your "life management" card was dealt out. You are intelligent, you are a likable person, but how can you explain the fact that you are always running late and, all too frequently, seem to be drowning in busywork? Although the following sad tale may not apply to you in all its particulars, there is probably something here that will cause you to grimace and sigh, "Oh God, it's me."

Leslie, our hero/heroine, tumbles out of bed at 8:30 A.M., stomach churning in panic, because that important appointment is set for 9:15, and the alarm didn't go off. Leslie dashes out of the house disheveled because there was no time to dress and groom properly, and because the shirt that goes with the plaid suit is missing as usual.

Breakfast is a sweet roll because Leslie has no time, naturally, for a real meal. But even under less harassed circumstances breakfast is a chore; who can ever find the eggs which are invariably hidden at the back of the refrigerator? And pulling the only decent frying pan out from under the pile of pots in the cabinet hardly seems worth the trouble.

Leslie arrives at the office barely in time for the appointment, which doesn't go as well as hoped, due to a general fuzziness of mind. The rest of the day assumes the same disjointed pattern: an important letter can't be found because of the mess on the desk; plans don't mesh with those of colleagues; and distractions abound, preventing any solid accomplishments.

Home again. Cooking a meal seems unendurable when utensils are piled into every nook and cranny of the kitchen. So once again, Leslie opens a can of tuna or orders a pizza.

Early evening might be a good time to get started on the income tax, but who knows what deductions to claim when the canceled checks have disappeared?

At last, a warm, relaxing bath to soothe away the tensions of the day. But relaxation turns to rage with the realization that all the towels are in the laundry.

And so to bed; with muscles taut, nerves jangling, and the sinking feeling that the whole thing is going to happen all over again tomorrow.

If Leslie's story applies to you at all, you must wonder what causes your wheels to spin in this way. The answer is complex, but there is nothing in your stars or your nature that dooms you to live out your days chafed and affronted on every side by such indignities. On the contrary, your innate capacity to organize is powerful indeed, but for a variety of complex reasons that instinctive capability was shortcircuited. The causes are primarily psychological, stemming from childhood; not to mention the constant challenge of coping with the mechanics of a highly sophisticated, complex world that our grandparents never knew.

You *are* capable, however, of setting your own life in order. Your inner drives toward order and clarity are much more powerful than the forces of chaos. Consider, for example, a major traffic circle and the experience of crossing it on foot or in a car. In your intrepid passage from one side to the other, whether as pedestrian or driver, you are spontaneously organizing a good deal of complex information: the velocity of the cars, their different angles of approach, their interrelationships with one another and with you. Managing this intricate situation signifies that you are highly successful at processing an assortment of information into a pattern that makes sense; the basic definition of organization.

Given the premise that we are all born with the inherent capacity to organize, what happened? I believe that many people get trapped in a sort of time warp in which they live out their present lives responding to forces that were in operation many years ago—as much as ten, twenty, thirty, or more years. The majority of people who are consistently (as opposed to only occasionally) troubled by the issue of order and disorder and by the logistics of managing their lives, are still, as adults, often living out guilty defiance of a childhood authority—usually a parent.

The process occurs in roughly the following way: an authority figure teaches a very young child that there is a way things "ought" to be. There is a "right" way to do things, and a "good" person is "disciplined" and "orderly."

This attitude toward life further affects the child when, as usually happens, the question of his or her own room becomes an issue. The constant refrain "Terry, clean up your room" becomes as maddening as fingernails scratching a blackboard. The child interprets this invasion of territory as an attack on his or her identity and autonomy. Sometimes this sense of assault is nothing more than imagination, but in many cases the child correctly senses a parent's need to control.

At some point defiance begins. The young person digs in his or her heels and mentally says, "I won't. I won't be orderly or disciplined." So he or she proceeds to make life chaotic in the belief that order means entrapment or loss of identity, and therefore disorder means freedom and affirmation of the self.

There is another factor that complicates this false assumption: guilt. As children or adolescents few people can defy their parents with a clear conscience. So even while one part of the personality may be affirming itself through defiance, the other part is saying, "I must be wrong, I must be bad."

The resulting burden exacts a heavy cost. A person moves from the imprisonment of someone else's rules to the imprisonment of a continuing functional disorder and, even more disheartening, to the deeper entrapment of a conflict in his or her own mind. In order to avoid this dilemma, people frequently assume conscious styles of living which seem to justify disorderliness.

One of these styles is "busy, busy, busy." Using this technique, a person becomes so frantically active with so many responsibilities, activities, problems and excursions, that there just isn't a moment to pull it all together.

Another style, not quite so widespread, is "free spirit." The "free spirit" is usually vaguely "artistic" or "creative," and thinks of organizing as the dullest possible activity for a person engaged in higher pursuits.

The most characteristic way people cope with the emotional bind of the order-versus-disorder conflict is by developing the attitude of "compliance/defiance." Many of my clients, for example, desperately want to be "right." They yearn to have their lives organized the way they "ought to be." That is compliance—the conscious acceptance of parental standards. Accordingly, they set specific goals of an exaggerated precision that would shame a computer scientist. Then, because these goals are unrealistic and often irrelevant to any genuine practical need, the person says, "The hell with it. I can't do it and I won't." That is defiance.

Guilty defiance no longer has much effect on your parents, but it serves effectively to block *you* from true freedom—true freedom, in the context of this book, meaning a system of *real* order, intrinsic to the person that you are, that liberates rather than constricts.

The specific elements of real order include a physical environment that is easy to move around in, easy to look at, and easy to function in; a simple technique for dealing effectively with the volume of paperwork and money business that we all must confront; and the development of a satisfying response to the fact that time is life, time is often money, and time is limited. This world takes shape as you develop a sensitivity to your own needs. In fact, this entire book is based on the proposition that there is no "correct" order, no right way to do things—whether setting up a file or a workroom or planning time—unless it is correct for you.

In other words, order is not an end in itself. Order is whatever helps you to function effectively—nothing more and nothing less. *You* set the rules and the goals, however special, idiosyncratic, or individualistic they may be. Then, using this book as a guideline, you can define your particular purposes and set up the practical systems to implement them. Figuring out your goals and purposes begins in the next chapter.

2

The Organizing Principle:

The key to straightening things out

All concepts of order, from the simplest system of closet arrangement to the most complex rocket technology, share one essential characteristic: an organizing principle. The idea behind the organizing principle is that any intellectual or practical system always contains a central pole, an essential priority, around which all the other components group themselves.

For example, when the Paris peace talks to end the Vietnam War first began there was a great fuss about the shape of the conference table, and the whole issue clearly grew to absurd proportions. But one of the parties to the talks felt the absolute need for a meeting at which all participants had the same rank, and thus the shape of the table became critical. People at a rectangular table have different status, depending on where they're sitting, but a round table confers no status—everyone is equal.

All the expected questions—what kind of table was most efficient, which tables were comfortable, what kind of table was available—were secondary to the real issue, the question of saving face. Once status was recognized as the organizing principle in designing the peace talks, the solution of which table to choose was obvious.

This example illustrates how the organizing principle functions as the focal point. If you determine what purpose you want to achieve, practical solutions will flow fairly easily.

Even more important, once the organizing principle behind an existing situation has been identified, you can decide whether it is the one that is right for *you*. If it is not, then you have the option of revising the principle.

Let's consider the organizing principle in terms of the psychological factors discussed previously. Probably, as your life became more and more complicated over the years, you have occasionally been able to step back and say to yourself, "I am being self-destructive. I've got to stop this right away." Whereupon you went through a period of intense, determined organizing which ended a day or two later when you discovered that nothing had really changed and you were right back where you started!

At that point the feeling of helplessness, of life out of control, must have been intense and painful. But if you look at this whole pattern with the idea of finding the organizing principle, the hidden factors may begin to reveal themselves. In all likelihood you are causing youself genuine pain in the service of a powerful theme, a powerful organizing principle: defiance of authority.

You have chosen defiance as your focus, and so long as it is in operation, you will always revert to the old pattern of defiance leading to chaos.

However, by recognizing that this outmoded, destructive organizing principle has been functioning quietly all these years, you are now free to bring it to the surface and change it—to devise a new principle more appropriate to your present life. Your organizing principle might then become: "The purpose of order in my life is my own ease and convenience—not domination by some impractical ideal." With that in mind as a basic point of reference, many changes become possible. Just as your previous actions were completely and spontaneously logical in terms of your old "defiance" motif, your newer mode of behavior will, after you accustom yourself to it, become completely logical in terms of the new "ease and convenience" theme.

And that's what this book is about. It will not only help you plan your personal business affairs or time or closets more efficiently, but it will also help you establish a permanent way of life fitted to your own desires and goals. However, there is a considerable leap from the grand abstraction of the organizing principle to the actual solving of a problem. First you have to understand very clearly just what the problem *is*. The rest of this chapter concentrates on how to pinpoint the problems in your life and bring them to manageable, solvable proportions.

It is not uncommon for clients to approach me with the cry, "Please straighten out my life." Their daily life seems overwhelming, and organizing it seems hopeless. Such people cannot see that specific, smaller difficulties must be resolved before the whole becomes manageable. Some clients, on the other hand, feel confronted by so many tiny problems that they are defeated by their very quantity.

The first step toward taking things in hand is to define just what a "problem" is. Never yet, in my experience, has a situation been so complex that it couldn't be unraveled.

To begin, provide yourself with a notebook—either looseleaf or spiral-bound—small enough to carry around with you. This notebook will become your "master list"—a single continuous list that replaces all the small slips of paper you're probably used to. Use the notebook to keep track of all errands, things to do or buy, and general notes to yourself about anything that will require action. This basic organizing technique is the first in a series of principles that will appear throughout the book highlighting the prime rules of organization.

Principle #1 **Use a single notebook for notes to yourself.**

Choose a time with no distractions and sit down with your notebook and pencil. List six elements in your life that need to be put in order. Forget about straightening out your life as a whole. Instead, focus on things like these:

> I spend so much time looking for kitchen utensils that cooking a meal takes hours. How can I make my kitchen "work" properly?
>
> I want to start woodworking again, but my books and tools are all over the house. What do I do to get them together?
>
> The living room is always a mess because I don't know what to do with all those magazines and newspapers I haven't read.
>
> I'm always running out of soap, toilet paper, and other household staples. How can I plan more effectively?
>
> It takes me forever to get ready in the morning and I'm always late for work. How can I streamline the "up and out" process?
>
> How can I plan enough time for special projects that I like to work on and still leave a comfortable margin for household, family, and other activities?

Substitute your own examples for mine, and you've completed the first step. If your mind tends to blur when you try to isolate problems, the "movie" technique may help. Take a deep breath and relax. Then close your eyes and mentally run through a typical day, letting it unroll like a movie. "I get up, brush my teeth . . ." and so on. When you come to a scene or situation that creates a problem, write it down. While you are screening your day's movie, remember that you may not be consciously aware of some problems but your mind and body are. If your stomach lurches or your muscles tighten or your head aches when you come to a particular scene, then you can be sure you have locked onto a problem.

If, for example, a twinge of tension occurs at the idea of brushing your teeth, perhaps you're always running out of toothpaste—a problem in maintaining an inventory control system for household supplies. Or, the toothpaste might be there, but the medicine chest is so jammed that a dozen other things fall into the sink every time you reach into the cabinet.

Write down each problem as you come to it, then shut your eyes again, relax, and continue. List no more than six problems, otherwise the list itself may overwhelm you!

This procedure of problem definition illustrates a fundamental rule of organizing—every life situation, no matter what it may be, can be divided into its significant parts. Stated as a principle:

Principle #2 **Divide up a complex problem into manageable segments.**

Some of the problems on your list will be fairly straightforward. A messy clothes closet, for example, is a small area with one function, and organizing it is a fairly simple procedure. But changing your morning ritual so that you're on time for work is a considerably more complex matter. It may involve changing your habits, revising your time schedule, reorganizing your bathroom or laundry system— or all of these things. Keeping Principle #2 in mind, the next step is to divide the *complex* problems on your list into more manageable units. These more complex situations usually fall into one of two categories:

1. *Physical areas: Rooms.* If an entire room needs reorganizing, you must first isolate its various problem areas. Stand in the doorway of the room and, choosing any corner at random, mentally block out an area about five feet square. Cast a sharp eye over every inch of that area to inspect it for "knots." In the living room, a knot might be a sloppy desk and work area, a disorganized wall unit with books piled in disarray, or an inconvenient and unappealing furniture arrangement. Whatever jars your nerves or sensibilities is a fit subject for reworking. List these specific "knot" areas on your master problem list under the general problem of which they are a part. Block out another five foot square area immediately adjacent to the first and repeat the process. Follow this procedure until you have checked the entire room and have a complete list of individual elements to work on.

2. *Processes or systems.* To break down a process or a system into its manageable parts, use the same movie technique, mentally running through the particular process that's giving you trouble. Each time you feel tension about an action or function, write it down. For instance, the stumbling blocks in the "up-and-out-in-the-morning" process might include some of the following: alarm clock rings too softly; cannot move quickly in the morning; don't have time to decide what clothes or accessories to wear; kitchen always messy so cooking breakfast is a chore.

There is one more very significant step that provides the bridge between defining the problem and finding the solution. On a scale of one to ten, rank each of the six major items on your list according to how much it irritates you. Stated as a principle:

Principle #3 **After articulating a small group of projects, rank them by number according to how *aggravating* they are.**

A problem that creates serious tension is a #1; one that could wait until next year is #10. Write the number next to each item on your list. This is a very important impetus to action. You may end up with two problems which are #1, two #2, one #5, and one #7. Do *not* try to arrange the problems 1, 2, 3, 4, 5, 6 in numerical order of importance. People tend to get so involved in figuring out which problem is fifth and which is sixth or whatever, that they lose sight of what they're trying to accomplish. If any of your six major problems can be subdivided as discussed on page 30, rank those subdivisions in the same way.

With this step of ranking, the process of establishing order is well and truly begun. The issues have been outlined, priorities have been set, and a foundation for action has been laid. All that remains before actually tackling the problems is to set a specific and regular time for organizing work. If you can't choose a good time, play a little game with yourself. Imagine that for the next several weeks you have a fixed appointment with yourself that you note in your appointment calendar as if it were a regular medical or dental appointment. Your "appointments" could be every day for an hour, or every day for fifteen minutes, or twice a week for two hours each, or an hour a week; whatever is practical in terms of other responsibilities and your own temperament. If you know you'll start getting jittery after half an hour, don't set a two-hour appointment because it will be "good for you" or you "ought" to. Instead, be kind to yourself and give yourself appointments that you know you can keep and handle.

But remember, these are firm appointments and must be kept, except in case of emergency. Making this commitment to yourself will be one of the smartest things you ever did.

Problem-Solving Checklist

Before you begin, review this checklist which summarizes your first steps.

1. Select and list in your notebook no more than six problems at one time.
2. Break the complex problems on the list into manageable units.
3. Rank the problems and their units according to aggravation level.
4. Turn to the appropriate section or sections of this book and solve the first #1 problem on the list; do not omit any units.
5. Go to the next #1 item, then the #2's, and so on until all the problems have been solved.
6. Choose another set of problems and follow the same steps.

PART TWO

Time and and Paperwork

3

The Basics of Managing Time

The productive use of time is ultimately a personal judgment; by your actions through the day, week, year, do you achieve the life that you want for yourself and your family? If so, your handling of time is basically sound. But if you constantly swing between periods of frantic and often useless activity and periods of inertia and procrastination, perhaps you should rethink your use of time—both in your daily life and in terms of your long-range ambitions. Before you can begin to organize your household and business systems effectively, you must learn how to use your time more efficiently and to your best advantage.

Planning the Day

There are three items essential to any effective daily time plan: a day-by-day appointment calendar; a pocket-size, spiral-bound or looseleaf notebook in which to jot down errands and other tasks as they occur to you (see chapter 2, page 28); and a daily To Do list, which puts the system in motion. Each morning or evening list ten things to do that day, compiled for the most part from items in the notebook, "follow-ups" in the calendar, plus one or two items from your "To Do" file folder (see Chapter 5, page 68) that require special attention. Rank each item on the list in the terms of its importance. Rather than a straight 1-to-10 listing, I recommend marking each item either #1 for high priority, #2 for medium urgency, and #3 for least urgent. The few minutes you spend each day making a To Do list will repay their value many times over.

Most To Do's should be specific and limited. The "Blackwell report," for example, may be too broad a prospect for one day; instead enter some of its components—"introduction" and "section on transportation"—as separate items on the list. Similarly, divide "clean the basement" into "tool corner," "pile of old furniture," and so forth. On the other hand, some To Do items might stand for a group of routine jobs: "errands," "phone calls," "routine correspondence."

In the *I Hate to Housekeep Book*, Peg Bracken offers an entertaining suggestion: play Time-Planner's Russian Roulette. On individual slips of paper, list some of the unpleasant jobs you've been putting off—"reorganize the first five file folders in the cabinet," "bring address book up to date," "reorganize the medicine cabinet,"—and, to make the game sporting, include some pleasurable activities—"go home early," "read a novel for an hour," "go bike riding,"—in a three-to-one ratio of pain to pleasure. Put the slips in an empty can, and on an off-day, draw one. Even if you draw a grim job, gambler's honor will get you started and there's always hope for next time.

As a general rule, however, the To Do list is the axis around which your day revolves. First, decide which chores might be more profitably delegated to other people—family, if at home, or colleagues. Then, to make your To Do list work *for* you, schedule the remaining tasks in terms of the practical factor, the biological factor, and the deadline factor.

The practical factor

Tasks such as report writing that require concentration should obviously be scheduled for hours when peace and quiet are available. Time of day and weather may also be factors. Ironing might be scheduled for the early morning, before the heat of the day. For the same reason, early morning may be the only comfortable time you have for gardening. Certain tasks require special equipment only available between certain hours; for example, there's often a backup on computer time.

First then, mark on your calender the To Do tasks that can only be performed at specific hours.

The biological factor

The concept of biological rhythm—the tendency, in its common definition, to be a "morning person" or a "night person"—is a fascinating and still relatively unexplored aspect of human experience. Every individual, during the course of a day, goes through a regular cycle of energy and acuity. Most people operate on "high" the first few hours of the morning, then dip in energy until a late afternoon low when energy ups again into early evening's "second high." Another drop between ten and eleven leads to bed.

Then there are the "night people" who have trouble adjusting to the nine-to-five world. They generally start with morning torpor, perk up around noon and through the late afternoon, and decline after dinner until about ten or eleven, when energy rises again making it hard to go to bed at a reasonable hour.

Whichever type you are, you may find that your efficiency increases strikingly if you arrange your tasks as much as possible around your own rhythms. A professional tennis player, for example, could not master a tricky new stroke although he practiced it every afternoon at three. One evening the player saw a TV documentary about biorhythm and decided to reschedule his practice session to his "higher" hour of 9:00 A.M. He mastered the new stroke on the second day and, as in all good tales, went on to win the tournament. He noted, "It was a strange sensation. At the 3:00 P.M. practices my body felt clumsy, and my judgment and depth perception seemed off. But the first day we started working at 9:00 A.M. I had a sense of confidence, and the second day I made it."

Take advantage of your own tempo similarly. You can check your own biorhythm by briskly exercising for five minutes in the morning and again in late afternoon. If you feel exhausted in the morning and invigorated in the afternoon, you may be a night person; if it's the other way around you're probably a morning person. Check your mental faculties as well. Work half of a challenging crossword puzzle in the morning and try the other half in the afternoon. Can you detect a difference in acuity?

When you know your individual pattern, draw up a rough plan and note your highs and lows. The pattern on the next page is fairly typical.

9:00 AM	to	noon	High gear
noon	to	4:00 PM	Fairly alert
4:00 PM	to	6:00 PM	Low gear
6:00 PM	to	10:00 PM	Fairly alert
	after	10:00 PM	Resting

Try to structure your daily To Do list according to your energy levels. "High" hours are most appropriate for top priority projects, projects requiring intense concentration or original thinking, or tasks that are unpleasant or stressful (for example, criticizing an employee). Routine jobs that you dislike qualify as "high" too. If starting dinner at 4:00 PM is a burden, organize dinner and set the table in the morning. The organizing projects suggested throughout this book should also be accomplished during "high" hours because they involve a change of habit, which can create stress.

Reserve "fairly alert" time for fairly routine work: meetings, ordinary correspondence, phoning, and so forth. During your very low time, plan for the next day, sign letters, do some professional reading, and so on. Try to relax a bit too. Chat with your colleagues, close your eyes for fifteen minutes, do several yoga exercises. During these periods, try to avoid situations—or people—that irritate you.

If you *must* attend the anxiety-producing staff meeting that is invariably called during your low time of 4:00 PM, give yourself a boost with a high-energy snack—a few spoonfuls of cottage cheese or some nuts and a glass of orange juice—about fifteen minutes before the meeting. Blood sugar levels, also a factor in mood and energy, can be raised by a protein snack.

The deadline factor and other scheduling tips

Knowing when to stop a project is as important as knowing when to start one. Everyone has different task toleration levels. One person can productively concentrate on a single project for four hours while another gets woozy and sloppy after an hour. And of course, different projects make different types of demands. Your personal responses are the key: when the sentence you've read three times makes no sense, when your muscles are aching—quit. The more effort you put into a project beyond the quitting point, the less value you are going to show for it. It is hard to judge the quality of your work when you are tired, so you may not even realize until the next day that your efforts were unproductive.

Because overwork leads to diminishing returns, crash programs are generally unsatisfactory, which is why careful planning that allows you to pace yourself—to drop what you are doing for a time and return later with renewed energy—is so important. (See page 36.)

Some people, on the other hand, who require pressure to work at top capacity really prefer to start a report due at 3:00 PM at 2:30. If that suits you, fine, *as long as* the documentation or information needed for the report is at hand. Scrambling for information at the last minute only causes panic.

Some people like to schedule their days very closely, from hour to hour. That's fine as long as you allow yourself flexibility. Reserve at least an hour a day for unexpected events and keep some time just for yourself.

Many time management experts advise that you try to drop the low priority, unimportant (#3) projects altogether, or postpone them into the indefinite future. But putting a project on the To Do list means it's on your mind, and ignoring it completely will create tension, which is even more nonproductive. I suggest that you reserve two or three hours a week, either in a block or divided up, devoted strictly to #3 projects. Divide the tasks into small segments; clean out only one shelf of the medicine chest, answer only the ten oldest letters.

Daily Time Plan Summary

1. Each evening or early morning list approximately ten items to accomplish that day. Compose the list from items in your notebook, entries in your calendar, and important projects in your To Do file folder.
2. Rank each item on the list #1, #2, or #3, depending on its importance or stress level.
3. Enter the To Do tasks in your calendar so that they correspond, to the extent practicable, with your biological rhythms.
4. Cross each item off the list as you complete it, and transfer unfinished items to the next day's list.

Eight Time Savers

Make better use of your hours with these time tips:

Barter. If a job is distasteful—such as balancing a checkbook or shopping—see if a friend or relative might be willing to take it on in exchange for a service from you. Although you are still spending time to perform a task, the general footdragging and timewasting involved in the effort to avoid a detested job is eliminated.

Make Use of Services. Rely on the professionals. Journalist Jane O'Reilly has written, "I once spent a week getting a vaccination certificate stamped. I wondered, does Elizabeth Taylor have to do this? No, and neither did I. The travel agent will get the tickets and see to the certificate, free of extra charge." (*New York Magazine*, January 17, 1972.) In fact, there are a lot of people who would like to help you out, usually however, for a price. If you work, pay the premium to engage home repair people before 9:00 AM or in the evening. Exercise professionals and hairstylists make house or office calls. Answering services will take phone messages for you. Messenger services deliver packages. One working mother opened a charge account with a taxi company to pick up and deliver laundry and packages, and take her children to their various appointments.

Take advantage of pick-up and delivery services offered by neighborhood merchants—the drugstore, dry cleaners, butcher and fish market—or, if possible, hire a teenager on the block for errands. Designate a spot for all items needing repair or cleaning. When you go out on a round of errands, check your To Do list and notebook to make sure that nothing is left out, and try to consolidate all your errands into one trip.

If you can afford it, a one-day-a-week cleaning person can be a boon. Draw up a list of regular assignments for your helper, and specify which products are to be used for what purpose. Within the first few sessions establish the standards of cleanliness you expect. An alternative that comes highly recommended is the professional cleaning service—a team of people, usually men, who come in on a contract basis once or twice a week to clean the whole house. They can also be hired as needed for specific tasks you loathe. Check the Yellow Pages under "Cleaning Services" or "House Cleaning." Only patronize firms that are bonded and insured.

Double up on time. Exercise while watching TV; do mending while chatting or helping the kids with homework. There are many small tasks that can be done at the same time.

Make use of bits of time. Plan small projects during waiting periods. Outline a report or pay bills while sitting in the doctor's office; polish silver while clothes are in the dryer; pick out a birthday card between appointments; make up the bed while waiting for the water to boil; make out your shopping list while riding on the bus. Most small chores can be accomplished in bits and pieces of time, as the following lists indicate.

What you can do in five minutes:
Make an appointment.
Make out a party guest list.
Dictate a short letter or write a note.
File your nails.
Water the plants.

What you can do in ten minutes:
Pick out a birthday card.
Order tickets for a concert or ballgame.
Repot a plant.
Handwash some clothes.
Clean up your desk.
Exercise.

What you can do in thirty minutes:
Skim a report and mark parts for later study.
Go through backed-up journals, magazines, and newspapers.
Work on a crafts project.

Plan Ahead. Set out clothes and breakfast utensils the night before. Check beforehand that you have all the necessary information to write a certain report. Make up a packing list for a trip a week or so in advance.

Pool Resources. Arrange a school pick-up pool, a car pool, play groups, and baby-sitting pools with other parents. Experiment with cooperative arrangements of various kinds.

Consolidate. Return all phone calls during a specific time period rather than responding to each one. Combine errands: when you're out grocery shopping, also pick up the shoes and take in the broken lamp. Also consolidate movement: for instance, pull up the sheets, blanket and spread on one side of the bed before crossing to the other. Keep file folders you use most often at your fingertips. Use rolling carts or mobile caddies whenever possible.

Labor-saving technology. Use labor-saving devices or appliances as much as possible. Take advantage of easy-care materials, no-iron fabrics, "no-show" carpets.

Planning

If you are working on a complex project, it is extremely important to pace yourself over the weeks or months that it takes. Consider, for instance, that you have been assigned overall responsibility in March for the December sales conference, an elaborate affair at a Florida resort hotel. The first thing to do—your #1 "To Do" the day the assignment is given—is to rough out the entire project. List all its main elements from start to finish—arranging a hotel, speakers, an agenda, audio-visual presentations—and list starting dates and deadlines for each component. Be *very* generous in your time estimates; double your first guess of how long each component will take.

List on a single sheet the starting and deadline dates for each component. They can, of course, overlap; you don't necessarily have to finish one aspect before going on to another. Then enter each starting and deadline date on your *daily* calendar. When you reach that page, you can then put that job or its subelements on your daily To Do list and follow up in the usual way.

Planning a less complex long-range job is easier, but the principle is the same. If, for example, you prepare your own taxes, select a deadline (preferably not too near the legal April 15 deadline), and list the components: buy a current tax guide, pick up supplemental forms if necessary, assemble documentation, do the actual calculations, fill out the form and send it in. Enter each component in your daily calendar at an appropriate date, and on that date mark it on the To Do list.

Long-Range Planning

Long-term planning should be determined by your goals and aspirations, whether they're specific ("I want to learn carpentry") or general ("I want to make a lot of money"). I don't intend to explore the question of defining your goals—several books on the subject are listed in the bibliography—but since the way you spend your time is ultimately a function of long-range goals, it's important to consider it, if only briefly.

The designer Milton Glaser challenged his students at the School of Visual Arts with a provocative assignment: design a perfect day for yourself five years from now. Not a fantasy day, but a real day that you would like to see yourself living in five years, one that is fully satisfying in terms of work, relationships with family and friends, and physical environment. The day can be an extension of your present life if that is essentially satisfactory, or a complete turn-about.

List your goals as that day reveals them. If you envision yourself in the country, put that down. If you see yourself speaking French in a cosmopolitan setting, list that. These are major goals.

Then identify the information you will need to decide whether to pursue these goals seriously. Those interested in country life might research farming, rural social life, and job opportunities. The French-speaking sophisticate might look into French classes, jobs available in travel, translation and diplomacy, and the qualifications that are required.

Once you've decided you're seriously interested in a particular goal, translate your goal list onto the To Do list. Begin the next day's To Do list with a concrete action to get things started; for example, registering for a class. It may also be time to drop some activities that are not leading toward your goal.

At least two or three times a week thereafter add a concrete, goal-directed item to your daily To Do list. Feel free to drop or revise your goals at any time if they seem unrealistic or incompatible with your chosen lifestyle.

Procrastination, Interruptions, and Irritations

Procrastination

Putting off or delaying work is, to a large degree, caused by setting impossibly high standards. Knowing the task simply cannot be done, you then attempt to ignore the work or put it off indefinitely. And justifying your inability to act by self-accusation—the "I'm just a lazy bum" syndrome—only locks you more firmly into a pattern of procrastination. You are, in effect, *instructing* yourself not to act! But there are ways to transmit new instructions that supercede the old ones.

You may be a victim of the *clear-the-boards* self-blocking technique: "I'll clean up the workroom as soon as I _____." The only answer is to force yourself, by an act of will, to put on blinders concerning other possible projects and take two baby steps. In the case of the workroom, lift one tool from the shelf, decide how to handle it, then lift another tool. When you've gone that far you will usually find the impetus to continue. If baby steps don't get you started, try again tomorrow. If you drop the job, *really* drop it; don't let it clutter your mind or your overwrought guilt mechanism.

The *big picture* is another major self-blocking technique. You have a closet to clean or a report to write, and you're going to *finish* what you start. Unfortunately, it's so overwhelming you don't even know where to begin. Bring your ideal into line with reality by assigning yourself segmented jobs, or divide the task arbitrarily by time. In an interview in *New York* magazine, Alan Lakein, time-management consultant, suggests punching holes into overwhelming projects by executing instant tasks that can be done in five minutes or less: drawing up a short outline of a report; making a phone call to get preliminary information.

There's another effective method for neutralizing the big picture problem—apply the "Well, as long as I . . ." technique: "Well, as long as I've got this file open I'll organize it." "As long as I've got the refrigerator open I'll wipe out one shelf." By the time you officially assign yourself the project you may find that it's practically done.

Perfectionism is a significant factor in procrastination: overorganization, overcleanliness, overconscientiousness. The supply closet, when you get around to organizing it someday, will be a model of perfection. Pencils will be laid out in parallel lines. Each box of paper will be separately labeled and at right angles to the pencils. It's exhausting to contemplate and it's not what organizing is about. If the mere thought of a job you're planning makes you tired, consider whether you might not be imposing standards that have more to do with an ideal of perfection than with functional efficiency.

If resistance to a particular task is overpowering, consider whether it is possible to drop it altogether. Can you hire someone else to do it? Or delegate it? Or exchange it for a service to someone else? If that is not realistic, it is worth taking some time to consider what the block might *mean:* Are you angry at your boss? Does the familiar chaos around you offer a kind of security? Do you dislike your job? Until you've solved the underlying problem, Lakein offers an interesting way to deal with the immediate inertia: sit quietly with eyes closed and say to yourself, "Well, I'm not going to do it, but this is what I would do if I were going to do it." Fantasize yourself going through the motions, and very often energy will start to rise.

Promise yourself a reward when you finish a job; a small reward for a small segment—a snack, a fifteen-minute yoga break, or a walk around the block—and a big reward for major accomplishments: a movie, a new pair of shoes, or even a day at the races.

Distractions and interruptions

Interruptions are one of the most intractable time management problems because they are, to some extent, uncontrollable.

If ringing telephones are your problem, an answering machine can be a boon. Choose a machine, however, that allows you a *very* short message. Many callers hang up during the thirty-or-forty-five-second message periods set by some brands. In lieu of a machine, ask friends to call only at certain times.

Actually, however, there are many ways to utilize time during extended phone conversations, especially if you have a shoulder attachment that frees your hands for taking notes, cooking, or simple housecleaning. It makes sense, in fact, to reserve some small chores—sewing buttons, writing checks, filing nails—specifically for times when you're on the phone. Keep extensions in the kitchen and work areas, and see that cords are long enough for mobility.

Family interruptions are to some extent unavoidable, but even young children can learn not to disturb a parent between certain hours, or when the door is shut, except for emergencies. Arrange your home so your children won't need you to take care of some of their everyday needs. For example, a four-year-old child can pour himself a glass of milk if both milk and glass are within reach.

If your children continually nag you about performing various tasks for them, analyze the action to see whether it can be made child-scale.

Sometimes it's necessary to remove yourself physically from distraction. The reading rooms of public libraries are soothing and conducive to concentration. Some libraries are equipped with individual study cubicles and have typewriters available for use. University libraries, which you can usually use if you register for one course, almost always have work areas.

Another way to get away from it all, without leaving home, is to rearrange your time. Some people go to bed early and set the alarm for midnight in order to have a few hours of uninterrupted work.

When interruptions are unavoidable, think of your project as a magnet that draws you back when circumstances allow. Don't emulate the dieter who lapses once and then says, "Okay, I failed, so I'll start stuffing myself again." After an interruption, return to your project with renewed steadfastness.

Small insults: protecting yourself from irritation

Eliminating or ameliorating the many regular irritations, the small insults, that affect your life can provide important results. For example, an unpleasant daily route to work through an industrial wasteland may prove depressing. Waiting in line is anathema to many people. Take a few minutes to analyze the irritants that stud your day, and then revise your schedule or your environment in whatever ways possible to at least soften their effect.

One client, a young journalist, consulted me because she was having trouble meeting deadlines. Her working system was good and didn't seem to account for the difficulties. But when she happened to mention how much she hated her trip to work on two subways and a bus, I suggested that the travel ordeal might be making her tense, and proposed an alternate route that eliminated one subway. The change took ten minutes longer, but was much more pleasant. Two weeks later the deadline problem was in hand. My client had not realized how much her entire attitude toward her work had been affected by her arduous commute.

Flexible thinking and analysis of alternatives is the key: if lines are a problem, plan bank visits to avoid the lunchtime crowd, or catch the early evening showing of a popular movie. One woman who was frazzled by rush hour crowds renegotiated her office hours to avoid travelling with crowds.

Physical decor or environment can have a strong psychological effect on your mood and work habits. Don't just resign yourself to the office you were assigned, adapt it to your pleasure; hang a few pictures, paint the walls, or re-cover the chair. Do as much as your employer will allow to make your working environment comfortable for *you*. The office is "home" for so many hours that it is well worth the time and money to make it as pleasant as possible. And you may find yourself working more efficiently in an atmosphere that *you* have designed to your taste.

4
Setting Up a Desk and Work Area

Paper handling, more than almost any other function, is dependent on a responsive physical environment— responsiveness defined as an appealing and practical location furnished with a comfortable working surface and sufficient supplies for every regular need. This "office" will become a permanent installation where the business of life is transacted—readily accessible, with all supplies, implements and files immediately at your fingertips, and where other household operations do not interfere.

Because establishment of a "personal office" is so basic, this chapter provides a step-by-step guide to pulling together an effective working environment.

Choosing the Location

The first thing to do is to select the place for your private office. In an ideal world, you could commandeer an entire room, but even if that is not practicable it *is* possible to choose a corner of your house or apartment that can belong to you alone.

Never select a corner that you don't like in the mistaken idea that it is "practical." A client of mine went through an experience that illustrates why. A freelance writer who works in his home, my client needed more extensive home office equipment and files than most people. The day I came to call he proudly showed me a room he had fitted up as a "real" office: executive desk, electric typewriter, filing cabinets, the works. It was very impressive. The problem, however, was that after putting so much money and equipment into the office, he didn't spend any time there.

First, it was removed from the main action of the household. Although privacy was essential, Mr. Davidson felt lonely without hearing his wife and four children in the background. It was important for him to feel part of his family, not isolated from it, and this elegant office was situated where no one else in the household had occasion to go. The other reason the office felt uncomfortable was that Mr. Davidson could not see outside. The room was built in such a way that he couldn't be refreshed by the sight of trees, grass, and children playing. Mr. Davidson had been sneaking upstairs to an empty room right in the center of the house, with a big window which looked out over the lawn and a wooded area. He could glance out at will while he sat and worked with a beat-up portable typewriter at a rickety desk.

What happened, of course, was that little piles of paper

sprouted throughout the house as he carried them from one location to the other or dropped them somewhere en route. Not to mention the fact that paper clips, stapler, stamps and other necessary supplies were never in the right place. His work habits were driving him crazy, and he had hired me to organize him back into his "real" office so that he could start to use it properly.

I convinced Mr. Davidson that this approach was the *wrong* one, that his beautiful, expensive office would never be the right place for him to work because he hated it. Instead of reorganizing the old office, I helped Mr. Davidson move everything into the room he really felt comfortable in. The moral of this story is that ultimately, the most practical location is the one that is agreeable to your spirit!

Few of us, however, have homes which provide so many alternatives. So the trick is to balance external realities—space, other people in the household, the amount of money available—against internal realities like those Mr. Davidson had to deal with—his need to be amongst his family, and his wish to see out the window. In order to reach some kind of workable decision as to location, ask yourself the following questions:

> Do you prefer a sunny room or a shaded one, and do you prefer to work in the morning or in the afternoon? These two questions are related because different rooms receive varying amounts of light at different times of the day.
>
> Do you like being near windows or do they distract you?
>
> Do you need isolation, or is it better for you to be near people?

Answering these three questions will immediately narrow your alternatives considerably. Now walk around your home and make a list of all the places which suit your preferences; for example, "windowed corner of living room," "unused breakfast nook."

Next, consider which of your alternatives makes you feel best. By this, I mean does the thought of working in a particular area make you feel internally "clear" and comfortable? Or is there a sense of internal tension, a nervous feeling? Number each alternative according to how "right" it feels to you. A really good feeling is #1, #2 is satisfactory, and #3 is just tolerable. Anything below a #3 should be forgotten immediately.

It would be ideal, of course, to settle immediately on your #1 choice, but *now* the concerns of convenience and practicality intrude themselves. To deal with them, here is a second set of questions to ask about each alternative:

Is there enough space for a desk and other equipment?

Is the general area structurally sound? If floors are sagging and walls are peeling, it doesn't sound like a very good prospect.

Is there a convenient electrical outlet and telephone jack?

Will this area be unobstructed during the times you want to use it, or will it get in the way of other household functions? Can these other functions be shifted to another time or place?

To help make the relationships clear, draw a rough chart in your notebook—similar to Figure 1—that lists the alternatives, with numbers to indicate their order of preference, and how well each of these questions rates with each alternative.

For instance, the breakfast nook has plenty of space, so that square would be marked "1." Structural soundness is adequate but not perfect, which would make that category about a "2." There is no electrical outlet or phone jack, so

Alternatives	Space	Sound-ness	Elec/phone	House-hold
1. Windowed corner of living room	X	1	1	3
2. Breakfast nook	1	2	X	3
3. Bedroom alcove	2	1	X	1
4. Storage room	1	1	1	1

Figure 1 Home office—Accessibility Chart

mark an "X" there. The "rest of the household" factor could be a problem. The nook isn't used to eat in, but the children have a tendency to run through the area as they go in and out of the house. They would have to be taught not to bother you when you are working, and to leave your supplies alone. So mark this square "3."

The storage room, on the other hand, fits every particular with a "1." So that's the answer, yes? No. According to the numbers on the chart, the storage room is last in preference. To choose it would involve yourself in Davidson's Dilemma. Instead, let's begin with the *favorite* alternative, and see how it intersects with the questions of convenience.

The favorite location is the windowed corner of the living room, but the space situation there is poor, so, sadly, that alternative gets crossed off. The next preference is the breakfast nook, and it will work. It's not perfect, you may have to do a little patching up and put in an outlet for a

lamp, but it will do. It is in the breakfast nook that preference and practicality *intersect*, to provide a point where
you can work while feeling good about it. This is an important rule to remember in choosing locations, or in designing any plan of action.

Principle #4   **When you have several alternatives to choose
from, select one which intersects at a point between your instinctive preference and the most "practical" alternative.**

Desk, Equipment, and Supplies

Once an area has been chosen, the next question is how to
get maximum use out of it. The first thing to do is measure
the entire area—length, width, and height—and mark the
dimensions in your notebook. You can refer to these measurements when you are trying to fit the right furniture
into your work space.

Next, how much money can you allocate to this project? The amount you spend will depend on how much furniture and supplies you have on hand, and how much you
have to buy. It is a good idea to set a limit, and keep a
record of what you spend so you don't go overboard.

The desk

A desk, of course, doesn't really have to be a desk. All
you really need is a surface to write on. You would be surprised at some of the arrangements people come up with.
One client, for example, is a theatrical agent who works out
of her apartment, or, more precisely, her bed. So far as she
is concerned, staying in bed until at least noon is more or
less an article of faith, but that doesn't mean she doesn't

work! She and I designed together a lap-desk arrangement that she could manipulate easily, write on, and store the basic supplies she needed. It was designed to meet a very special situation. Your own desk should be just as carefully suited to your needs.

Look around your home to see if there is a suitable desk or table which would fit into the dimensions of the work area. If you find a table, it should be sturdy, high enough to write on comfortably, and large enough to hold various implements on its surface. Also, if you choose a table, as opposed to a fully fitted desk, space must be allocated for a filing cabinet, and possibly for a typewriter table.

If you can't find a desk or table in your home, buy a desk. It is an investment you won't regret. There are so many different kinds of desks available that you should have no trouble finding one which has the practical characteristics of office models, but is still attractive in your home. Here are the specifications to keep in mind:

1. *Writing surface.* Like the ideal table, your desk should be sturdy and comfortable to use, with a writing surface that doesn't wobble.

2. *Place for supplies.* A modern office desk is usually fitted with a special drawer for stationery, carbon paper and the like, with stationery sections inserted at approximately a 45° angle. This is ideal, but you can do without the specially constructed drawer if there is at least one large drawer in which paper and envelopes can be kept in folders. There should also be a shallow drawer with compartments for paper clips, rubber bands, and odds and ends.

3. *Files and records.* A home office seldom has need for more than one file drawer, or sometimes two. If your desk has at least one drawer big enough to contain "letter size" (11¾" x 9½") file folders, all your files will probably be comfortably accommodated.

4. *Typing platform.* If you have a typewriter and plan to use it in your work area, try to get a desk with a built-in platform for the typewriter to rest on.

When space is particularly tight, consider the "Mini-Office," * a compact cabinet that opens out into a fully-fitted desk complete with space for typewriter, paper supplies, etc.

Other furniture and equipment

A desk with all these accoutrements is perfect, but if your basic piece of equipment is a table, a partially outfitted desk, or a slab over two filing cabinets, then you may need various supplementary items to store everything:

Place for stationery, carbons, yellow pads, envelopes, etc. I use a portable metal stationery rack, of the kind available in office supply stores. It has several small open drawers, and can hold different kinds of paper supplies.

File cabinet. A two-drawer file cabinet, preferably of "letter size" width, should take care of most storage requirements. You can stand it in a closet if you don't want it visible, but file cabinets are now made in pretty colors to fit home decorating schemes.

Tray with compartments for small articles like pens, paper clips, and rubber bands. Any office supply store has these trays in a variety of materials and colors.

Chair. Don't choose a chair already in use somewhere else in the house. Your work area should have its own chair—one that is comfortable to sit in. Swivel

---

* A Norwegian product distributed in the U.S. by Norsk, Inc., 114 E. 57th Street, New York, N.Y. 10022

chairs are particularly useful because you can turn from one position in your work area to another without getting up.

Here is a miscellany of storage ideas:

Use an extra bookcase shelf for portable typewriter, some files, baskets of supplies.

Decorative objects make good storage containers. A ceramic mug looks attractive holding pencils and pens.

Paper, pencils, and supplies can be kept in stackable plastic or vinyl storage cubes kept under the desk. Or use storage bins on runners which, in effect, make drawers.

Expand on the classic in/out box with stackable plastic boxes that can be added on indefinitely. There is a small style for stationery and papers, and a larger one—actually meant to be a vegetable bin—for stacks of magazines and newspapers.

Wall organizers—molded plastic pieces that hang on the wall—are helpful for pads, pens, calendar, and other current supplies.

Supplies

This section is basically a checklist outlining the kinds of things you need to make your work area function properly. Wherever possible I suggest that you buy items in quantity—enough for current use plus extra for backup stocks. For example, a full box of 500 sheets of white paper, a full box of copyset carbon paper, and two boxes of pens will last for a good long time. Backup stock can be kept in a closet, or some place away from the work area if your storage space is limited. As you reach the bottom of your supplies, note the items in your notebook and pick up new stocks when convenient.

Address book or rolodex.

Appointment calendar. This item is a very important part of the personal business system. Ideally, the calendar should be small enough to carry around with your notebook, as well as for use at your desk. If you look hard enough in stationery and office supply stores, perhaps you can find a combination notebook and calendar that isn't too bulky to carry around in your briefcase or handbag. In any case, the "date" squares should be large enough to list appointments comfortably.

Bulletin board. If it fits into your work area, a bulletin board is a good place to collect notes and reminders to yourself. A few squares of stick-on cork, available in any hardware store, will do very nicely. Attach notes with push pins.

Carbon paper. I recommend that you make a carbon copy of any business letter you write. The most convenient kind is "copyset" carbon paper—the backup paper is attached to the carbon, which is torn off and thrown away after use.

Desk lamp.

Dictionary.

File folders. Letter-size folders are easier to handle than the wider legal size. In either case I suggest "third cut" folders, in which the stick-up tabs are staggered so they don't block each other from view.

Letter opener.

Marking pens. It is useful to have on hand a few marking pens in different colors.

Paper clips, regular size and oversized. A small box of each.

Pencil sharpener. If you are a serious pencil user, I suggest a desk model sharpener, either manual or one of the handsome electric ones.

Pencils and pens.

Postage scale (a small one). For oversized mail.

Rubber bands. Buy a small box of mixed sizes.

Rubber stamp and ink pad. This item is optional, but it is a nice idea. To eliminate the need for letterhead stationery which is expensive, any office supply store can make up a stamp with your name and address.

Ruler.

Scissors.

Scratch paper. Buy some lined yellow pads for drafting letters and writing down thoughts.

Scotch tape and dispenser.

Stamps. Aside from regular stamps, keep the appropriate postage on hand for special mailings if you do them regularly.

Stapler, staples, staple remover.

Stationery and envelopes. For most purposes 8½ by 11-inch plain white paper (with rag content for a better quality) and matching business-size (#10) envelopes are fine. Buy smaller notepaper also, for personal use. If you use letterhead stationery, get some plain white paper anyway for second sheets and general purposes. Also buy some oversized manila envelopes if you have occasion to mail out thick documents, magazines, etc. Jiffy bags, which are padded to protect fragile packages, can be useful as well.

Telephone. You won't believe how much easier life will be if you install an extension right at your desk.

Typewriter. This item is optional. But if you can type, or want to learn, I strongly recommend the typewriter as a way to increase your efficiency. A reliable portable model will serve most purposes. If it's not convenient to leave the typewriter permanently out on the desk, or on a table to the side, get a model that's light enough to put away easily; some portable models are quite heavy.

Typewriter correction paper.

Wastebasket.
White-out fluid.

Once you have furnished the supplies, the next chapter discusses how to put them to good use.

5

Paper:
What to do with it, how to file it, when to throw it away

From my experience, paper—letters, bills, communications and information of infinite variety—is the single greatest human irritant. And yet, there are only three things that can be done with a piece of paper: it can be thrown away; something can be *done* about it, such as writing a letter or making a phone call; or it can be temporarily put away. This holds true for a private individual conducting a modest amount of personal business or for IBM; IBM just has more paper to handle.

The difficulties of handling paper arise when one must choose which have value and which do not. It is not uncommon to feel that one's life is somehow bound up with keeping papers and files, and the idea of throwing anything out can be quite frightening.

I remember one client, an elderly woman whose small New York apartment was massed with the paper accumulations of a lifetime. She wanted desperately to clear out this stifling undergrowth, and yet when I came to her home she was trembling and close to tears. "I just know," she said, "that you're going to take my past away. My life, my history, is in these papers."

I explained to her that what I try to do is help people choose what has value for them; and sentimental or historical value has just as much meaning as financial value. I would never force this woman to throw away anything; I would simply help her to make those value/nonvalue distinctions in order to make her life more orderly.

As we worked, my client realized that much of the material stacked up in her apartment had no meaning to her. We kept the papers that really did contain her life history; other musty documents that she was saving because somehow, someday, one of them might "come in handy," we threw out. By the end of that day she had learned how to discriminate between valuable and valueless papers, and thus was able to throw many away with a clear conscience.

Other people may not have accumulated great masses of paper, but they have never learned how to *use* paper as a means of carrying on the business of life. That is another purpose of this chapter: to teach you how to let paper assume its true function as a cue and a trigger for action, not as a smothering weight in your life.

In order to learn this lesson, let's trace the fortunes of an imaginary day's mail. We will follow this batch of mail through all the stages of its life, until, by the end of the chapter, you will be able to face any mass of paper, big or small, with the confidence that you know how to integrate it into your life.

You have just picked up the daily mail; before glancing at it, immediately take the mail to your office area. Your schedule may be such that you can't work on it now, which is fine; in that case, just drop it off on your desk. Do *not* sit down on the living room couch and start opening letters. Opening mail elsewhere than your designated "office" adds an extra physical action and an extra thought process. Once you are surrounded with the torn envelopes and the contents of the mail, you will have to gather it all up again and take it to your desk for sorting and action. Or, more likely, you *will not* take it back to the desk and sort it. Rather, everything will look such a mess that your stomach will begin to tighten and you will push that day's mail— and perhaps several others'—out of sight.

By taking the mail to your desk, you are "intersecting" with the system designed precisely to deal with that kind of activity. In fact, this "intersection" idea applies to many different contexts. This particular variation of it can be stated:

Principle #5   **Always carry out actions in a location that intersects with the system designed to deal with those actions.**

Stage One: Sorting it Out

Now you are sitting comfortably at your desk with a stack of mail before you. There are fifteen pieces:

1. Electric bill.
2. Department store bill.
3. Personal letter to you.
4. Personal letter to your spouse.
5. Letter from your lawyer asking you and your spouse to set up an appointment to discuss some property you have just bought.

6. The deed to the property is also enclosed.
7. Notice of sale at local camera store.
8. Invitation to cocktail party next week.
9. Flyer from your Congressperson telling you how well he/she is doing in Washington D.C.
10. Local repertory theater schedule for this coming season.
11. Letter from local Boys Club asking you to contribute time toward putting together the annual fund-raising fair.
12. Notice from the doctor that it is time for your child's annual polio booster.
13. Magazine subscription renewal notice.
14. Two magazines.
15. Newspaper.

These miscellaneous bits of paper all fall into one of the three broad categories outlined at the beginning of the chapter: those to be thrown away; those to be acted upon; and those filed for reference. You will need the following "places" in order to sort your paperwork:

A wastebasket.
File folders marked:
    Things to do.
    To file.
    Your spouse's name (if you have one).
    Financial.

The two last categories are special but necessary subdivisions of the "things to do" category. You can use pretty baskets or boxes instead of file folders, but I've found that the folders are the most practical. They can be put away out of sight in your file drawer, or you can leave them out on the desk in one of those standup organizers.

Let's begin by tracking through the pile piece by piece:

1. Electric bill. This goes into your "Financial" folder. All documents related to money should be placed in

the financial folder for handling all at one time. This includes bills, bank statements, cancelled checks, investment notices, etc.

2. Department store bill. Also put into the "Financial" folder.
3. Personal letter to you. After you have read it, assuming you plan to reply, slip it into your "Things to do" folder.
4. Personal letter to your spouse. Put into the folder marked with your spouse's name.
5-6. Letter from lawyer and deed. This is actually two items. The letter requires discussion with your spouse so it goes into the "Spouse" folder. The deed is slipped into the "To file" folder or basket.
7. Notice of sale at local camera store. Many people have a terrible time deciding what to do with miscellaneous pieces of paper like this one. Because there may be some ambiguity involved, let's go through the alternatives pretty thoroughly. The question to ask yourself is "Do I care?" Does someone else in the household care? Consider these possibilities:

   a. Your spouse is a camera buff. Then, the "Spouse" folder seems like a good place.
   b. *You* are a camera buff and there are some supplies you have been meaning to buy. Put the notice in the "Things to do" folder.
   c. You do photographic work, but don't need anything now. If the name and address of the store is valuable information to you, put the notice in the "To file" folder.
   d. You don't do photography, have never done photography, don't think you ever will do photography, but someday you just might want to know about this store. Then the notice goes out. Yes, out. This information has no current meaning for you; to save it is to clutter up your life uselessly. If you ever do need a camera store, go to the yellow pages or get suggestions from friends.

Remember that saving things for a rainy day, or because they might come in handy sometime, is self-destructive. Fear is the driving force that causes people to cling to things that have no value to them. Learn to master that fear by making decisions about what has real value for you and what doesn't. Then you will be well on your way to getting organized!

8. Invitation to cocktail party next week. Is this something to be discussed with your spouse? If so, the Spouse folder is where it goes. If you yourself make the social decisions, then slip the invitation into your "Things to do" folder.

9. Flyer from your Congressperson. Do you care? Again, this is the important question. If you are actively involved in politics, then you might indeed want to read it and even save it to follow an issue you are particularly concerned about. If you want to keep it, the information goes in "To file." But if it is of no special interest, then out it goes.

10. Local repertory theater schedule. Again, does this information have value to you? If so, you might want to make plans with your spouse. In that case, the schedule goes into the "Spouse" folder. Or perhaps you perhaps you will buy some tickets just for yourself, or yourself and some friends. Then, put it into "Things to do." If there is no genuine interest—out!

11. Boys Club letter. If this is a personal letter that you have to deal with in some way, it is a "thing to do." But if it is a form letter, you can throw it out if you're not interested.

12. Polio booster. A "Thing to do."

13. Magazine subscription renewal. If you are not going to renew, throw it out. If you are, the notice is a "Thing to do."

14. Two magazines. Keep all your unread magazines in one place and make sure they are read and thrown

away regularly. If you find that a particular magazine is accumulating unread, then stop the subscription.

15. Newspaper. Basically the newspaper should go into the "Things to do" file because it should be read quickly. People respond to their daily newspaper in different ways. Most read it and get rid of it, but some hold on to their newspapers. I've worked with many a client whose stacks of newspapers blocked out light and air. This is one instance where you must be extremely firm about throwing out. Get rid of every newspaper right up to yesterday's if you haven't read it, and add "no time to read the newspaper" to your list of "life problems" to be solved!

There is also the question of clippings. Newspapers provide much useful information about stores, services, travel, restaurants, health information, etc. By all means clip anything interesting, and put your clippings in "To file."

Once you get the hang of the sorting process, it won't take even half as long to do as it takes to read about it. Here is a straightforward summary of what we have just done. You can consult it every time you work at your desk, until the steps become automatic:

Sorting checklist

1. Divide the mail according to what has interest and value to you and what does not.
2. Throw away the "no interest" pile.
3. Divide what you're saving into reference piles and action piles. Put the "reference" pile into the "To file" box or folder.
4. The "action" material can be divided still further. Things having to do with spending money—bills, banks, financial statements—go into the "Financial" folder, which is handled once a month. There is a spe-

cial folder for things to discuss with your spouse; otherwise, all "action" materials go into the "Things to do" folder.

Stage Two: "Things to Do" and Follow-up

Once everything has been sorted out and set into its appropriate folder, you are ready to begin actual work.

If your spouse is available, I suggest dealing with that folder first, so those items can be integrated into your main "Things to do." If that is not possible, be sure to go over the folder with him or her before your next "office hours" session.* Then the items that require more work—ordering theater tickets, for example—can be slipped into the "Things to do" file for the next "office hours" session, and the rest can be thrown away or put into the "To file" folder.

Now take out your "Things to do" folder. Make those phone calls, write those letters, do whatever is called for. To make it clear how this works and how to tie it in with the other elements of your paperwork system, let's deal with a few of the items from the morning mail that landed in the "Things to do" folder.

Personal letter to you.

Camera store notice.

Cocktail party invitation.

Repertory theater schedule.

Boys Club letter.

Polio booster notice.

---

* Set a regular time for "office hours" that fits into your existing schedule. Two hours a week is sufficient for most people, either in one sitting or divided up. Don't try to catch up on backed up organizing work in this time period; this is for current business. Go through the older materials in the time period you chose for organizing (Chapter 2, page 38).

Magazine subscription renewal.
Newspaper, read and check for clippings.

After you have answered the personal letter you may want to save it, in which case the letter goes into "To file." Otherwise throw it out. As for the camera store notice, make a note to yourself in your notebook (which is always with you, of course!) to go to the camera store during your next shopping trip. Then if the notice itself contains some information you want or need, tuck it in the notebook or stick it up on your bulletin board.

The invitation to the cocktail party requires two actions: an RSVP and, assuming you plan to go, marking it down in your appointment calendar. Similarly with the theater schedule, send for your tickets and mark the dates on the calendar. For the polio booster notice, call your doctor and make an appointment for your child to get his or her shot, mark it on your calendar, and then put the notice in "To file."

There is one other area we haven't mentioned yet. What do you do when you plan to initiate a project? Suppose, for instance, you start thinking about getting a cost estimate for turning the garage into a family room. Right then and there, jot the idea down in your notebook. Thus, your office hours will also include, besides responding to mail that comes in, checking your notebook for self-initiated projects requiring your attention. When you decide to get in touch with the contractor about an estimate, write, don't phone. Phone requests are lost very easily because not everyone is as organized as you are going to be! Keep a carbon copy of the letter itself and put it into a new file folder labeled "Pending" or pin it on the bulletin board. Then (*this is really important in order to keep your system flowing*) mark on your appointment calendar a date by which you might reasonably expect a reply. If, for example, you mail

the letter on Monday the 18th, and estimate that the contractor needs a week and a half to think the thing over,
mark "contractor?" on your calendar for Wednesday the
27th. This cryptic question will indicate that you should
follow up if you haven't heard anything by that day.

If the contractor does get in touch, make notes of any
discussion on the carbon copy of the letter, mark any appointments you make on the calendar, and put the letter in
"To file."

"Things to do" checklist

1. Go through each piece of paper in the "Things to do"
   pile and respond to it in some way—write a letter,
   make a phone call, whatever is appropriate.
2. "Track" each piece of paper, after you have worked on
   it, into its proper channel: wastebasket, "Pending," or
   "To file."
3. If there is to be any follow-up mark that in your calendar.
4. Check your notebook for projects that you want to set
   in motion, and do whatever has to be done.
5. Check the appointment calendar for any notices scheduled for that day, and follow up.

After a while this rhythm will come so naturally to
you, you'll wonder how you ever had trouble with it before.

Stage Three: The Fine Art of Filing and Finding Again

Once you've taken care of "Things to do," all that remains
is to file whatever remains in the "To file" folder. The idea
of filing frightens some people; they feel they will never be

able to find anything again. Don't let such fears get the better of you. Keep in mind that we are simply dealing with pieces of paper that are going to be put away precisely in order that they *can* be found again.

The process is simple. Examine each piece of paper, establish its reason for being in the file (which gives the clue for categorizing it), and then physically place the paper in one or another labeled file folder. The trick is, of course, to file things under the right labels so that you can find them again. Let's follow this procedure with that imaginary pile of mail that ended up in the "To file" folder:

1. Personal letter. Personal letters are usually saved because the writer's correspondence has emotional value for you. How do you categorize this piece of paper? It is a *personal letter*. The first clue to setting up a file folder is to determine the *broadest* category that a piece of paper can belong to. Nine times out of ten, that broad category is perfectly sufficient to label any file folder. In this case, take out a file folder and label it "letters" or "personal letters." Then slip the letter into the folder, and that's it.

Let's say, though, that you have stacks and stacks of personal mail to keep—much too much to fit into one folder. Then you might want to subdivide the letters into more than one category. One alternative is to do it by date: "Letters '79," "Letters '80," "Letters '81." Or, you might label folders with the individual names of the persons who sent the letters. Now we get into a slightly confusing area, the kind of point that throws people off. Should these folders be labeled "Letters, Susan," or "Susan, Letters," or what? If the *person* is the relevant subject, then the folder should be labeled "Susan," or "Michael" rather than "Letters, Susan," or "Letters, Michael." If Susan or Michael is so important that there's a whole folder's worth of letters from each of them, there will probably be other materials about Susan or Michael that will go into the same folder. In other words, if you ask the question, "What is the file about?" and the answer is the *person* not "letters," then the name should go on the label.

2. Property deed from the lawyer. This could be confusing. Should the deed be filed under the name of the lawyer? Or, supposing this specific property is located in a little town called Eastgate, perhaps it should be filed under "Eastgate"? Again, what is this piece of paper about in its *broadest* terms? The answer is "property." Unless you have a great many holdings indeed, the chances are that any correspondence or documents about all of your property will fit into one single folder.

Don't forget the accompanying letter sent by the lawyer. Right now it is out to be discussed with your spouse, but when the letter is ready to be filed, I would suggest slipping it into the same folder as the deed. This brings to mind another tip for filing: papers connected to each other are filed with each other.

But why not use the name of the lawyer or law firm? If they are your regular attorneys you may already have a correspondence file headed with the name of the firm. In that case, shouldn't this property material go into that folder, on the principle of unifying materials as much as possible? Good thinking, but on the whole I recommend that you set up a "property" folder. You will probably, over time, accumulate material concerning this piece of property from sources other than the lawyer—tax assessments, contractors doing improvements, etc.—so the focus of the file is the property, not the lawyer. However, the argument in favor of filing the deed under the lawyer's name is a good one and could give rise to legitimate debate. I suggest that you use a device known as a "cross-reference" to draw your attention from one file to another. Thus, in this particular case, write a little note saying "Material concerning property in 'property' file," and slip the note into the file headed by the attorney's name.

3. Camera store notice. In this case, "photography" is the most obvious and broadest answer to the question, "What is this piece of paper about?" That heading makes the most sense, *so long as there are other materials on photography* to keep it company. The other materials might include a "how-to" article on taking pictures in dim light, or a clipping discussing the relative merits of different types of cameras, but no item should ever repose alone in a file. The point is to devise *broad categories*.

If there are no other file materials concerned with photography choose the next broad category it might fit into. It is also a store, which gives us the broader, useful heading of "stores" or "shopping"—whichever term is more comfortable for you.

4. Flyer from Congressperson. If your interest in politics is vital enough to warrant saving the flyer, the obvious choice for a file heading would be "politics." Or, if you plan to save the flyer for its discussion of a specific issue on which you are collecting other material, such as "environment," or "foreign policy," then the flyer fits most comfortably into the folder headed by the name of the issue.

5. Notice about polio booster. Here the choices are pretty obvious: one option is the broad heading "medical," while the other one seems to be the name of the child. In this instance, there are two equally clear-cut answers to the question, "What is it about?" The notice is as much about "medical" as it is about the child. Simply choose the alternative which triggers an association for you, and then stick to it consistently over time.

Thus, if you choose "medical," the entire family's medical history would be kept in that folder; that would be the subject. If you prefer to keep the medical information in an individual folder for each member of the family, it would be placed in the same folder with other papers having to do with that individual, including letters. It doesn't matter, as long as you follow a consistent path one way or the other.

6. Newspaper clippings. As a tip to lessen your reading load, pick out the specific magazine or newspaper articles you want to read from the table of contents rather than by flipping through the whole issue, which invariably means you will end up reading the entire issue. For the sake of discussion, let's suppose you have cut out five articles to be filed for reference. Here's how to file them, always remembering that central question, "What is the piece about for me?"

a. An article on how much Vitamin C to take if you feel a cold coming on. The "umbrella" term here is "health" and that is what the file should be headed. If you are in the habit of cutting out articles like this make a separate folder for this subject. Otherwise put the clipping in your medical folder dealing with other medical matters.

b. An article giving tips on hotels in Tahiti, where you've always wanted to go. Why not "travel"?

c. A piece on craft schools. This subject is a little ambiguous and will need some thinking through. If you have various other materials on the broad subject of crafts, then this seems like the obvious heading. But if you're in a general self-improvement mood and are cutting out lists of classes in a variety of different areas, then maybe "schools," "instructon," "classes," or some related term that evokes an association from you is the answer. Or maybe "self-improvement," if that term covers a variety of different items for you.

A client of mine came up with a fine idea for problems of this kind. We had been going through her files, and eventually collected a little batch of items that we couldn't decide what to do with—things like a list of craft schools, instructions on making a lamp out of an old bottle, a few books she planned to read one day. There weren't enough items to make individual files, but we still had to make some decision—and *not* "miscellaneous" please! Any file labeled "miscellaneous" is going to prove a horror. My client mused for a moment and then said, "how about 'aspirations'? These are all my aspirations for the future." It was perfect for her, and it might be perfect for you.

d. Review of a newly opened nightclub. How about "entertainment"?

e. An article on where to find the best selection of sweaters. Put this item in a "stores" or "shopping" folder, the same one that contains the camera store notice. If you find that folder is becoming too bulky with items on clothing, you might want to take those items out and set them up in a separate folder called "clothing" or "fashion." Similarly, if you are a woman, you might find that quite a few of your shopping items have to do with cosmetics, hairdressers, etc., and in that case you might want to make a separate "beauty" folder, or include beauty items in "fashion." Sit quietly for a moment and let yourself respond to the association your mind makes spontaneously. Follow it through and you'll be fine.

One final tip about your personal filing system: it is usually a good idea to file every folder in strict alphabetical order by its heading, and avoid any subgroupings that may occur to you. One client, for example, proposed to collect all the folders concerned with the members of her family— Susan, Mary, Tom—and group them in one "family" section. I advised against that plan, and recommended that "Susan" just be filed under "S," "Mary" under "M," and so on. This kind of overarching category is not usually a good idea because, in order to find the file again, you have to remember both the major heading *and* the subheading.

Filing checklist

Here is a filing checklist which can be used to develop a system from scratch; to revise an existing system that isn't working well; or to maintain effective files on a day-to-day basis.

1. Gather together all materials to be filed so that they are all in one location.
2. Have a wastebasket or box for trash handy, along with file folders, labels, and pen.
3. Pick up the item on the top of the pile (or the first paper in the first folder if you are revising an existing file) and decide whether this item has value for you. If it does not, throw it away. If it does, go on to the next step.
4. If the piece of paper is worth retaining, ask yourself the question, "What is this about *for me?*" and choose a folder heading for it.
5. Now label the file folder and slip the piece of paper in. Here are some of the most typical headings for a home file:
   Beauty
   Decoration
   Entertainment
   Fashion
   Financial
   Health
   Household
   Letters *or* Correspondence
   Medical
   Property

Restaurants

Services (household services, such as plumbers, electricians)

Taxes

Warranties & Guarantees (for appliances, television sets)

6. Pick up the next piece of paper and go through the same procedure, the only variation being that this new piece of paper might well fit into an already existing file, rather than one with a new heading. Consolidate as much as possible.

7. When your mind begins to blur, stop filing for that day.

8. Assemble your pile of file folders and put them in strict alphabetical order.

9. Put your alphabetized folders into your file drawer, prop them upright with the sliding support in the drawer, close it, and you are finished for this session.

10. Finally, to maintain your file once it is established, each time you consult a file folder, riffle through it quickly to pick out and throw away the dead wood.

The desk check

At the end of your office hours, or at the end of the work day, assure that papers won't go out of control again and make ready for tomorrow by carrying out the three-point desk check:

1. Are all "To do" papers in the "To do" file?

2. Are all "To file" papers in the "To file" box?

3. Any papers left out on the desk are as yet untracked. Track them before you leave. Any paper you're unsure of means that some decision has to be made—even if the decision is only whether or not to throw it away. Making a decision is an act, and therefore the paper is a "To do."

Setting Up a Paperwork
System From Scratch

You now have a good background in all of the basic ways to handle the flow of paper in your life. What about those poor souls who have to start from scratch, whose lives are currently so disorganized that they have nothing but a bare desk surface and some basic supplies? First, gather together all your paperwork from its various locations throughout the house. Ferret out those piles of magazines, canceled checks, clippings, and documents from closets, drawers, the kitchen table, and wherever they can be found. Whatever and wherever your paper may be, pull it *all* together and collect it at your desk or in your work area.

Don't panic if your papers fill a carton or two or five. These cartons may look as if they will take months to go through, but they won't. The longest home office job I *ever* had took only three days!

Once the material is collected, make up the basic file folders we've discussed—Things to do, To file, Spouse, Financial, and Pending. Then start out with the top of the pile, just as we did with the "daily mail" example, and take care of each item. One word of caution—don't work too long at one sitting on this job. Your mind will become fuzzy. Just make sure that you keep those regular appointments with yourself; those parts of the day that you have promised to devote to getting your life together. You will be surprised at how quickly the papers move out of their cartons and into the wastebasket or their new homes. In no time at all you will bring order and clarity out of chaos.

Addendum: Addresses and Special Dates

Two questions that people ask me over and over are: how do you keep track of the stores or services you may someday need? and how do you remember birthdays and special anniversaries from year to year?

The solution to the first problem is to set up your personal classified phone directory. Suppose you collect antiques. List "antique dealers" all together under "A" rather than under the names of the firms. Similarly, "furniture restorers" would go together under "F." It's generally a good idea to use a different address book for your personal "yellow pages" rather than combining them with your personal address book. One client, instead of using an address book, bought a handsome "Rolodex" with plastic pockets— actually intended for photographs—and slipped the firms' business cards into the pockets. If you always think of a firm by its name, then list it that way with a cross-reference to its function. You might, for instance, enter "Acme Cleaners" under "A," and then enter under "C," "Cleaners—see Acme."

To remind yourself of birthdays and anniversaries, make up a master list. Then enter each individual date on your calendar, and staple the list itself to the last page of the calendar. Make a note to yourself in late December to "transfer birthday list and dates" on next year's calendar. This can be carried over from year to year.

PART THREE

Money

6

The Master Plan

"I don't know where the money goes. I make a fair income, I don't buy custom-made suits or mink coats—so why am I always just this side of the poverty line?" This is the Song of the Plaintive Consumer. Spontaneous extravagance, however, is generally not the problem. More to the point are the nagging day-to-day questions you can't answer: "Where is my money going?" "Why can other people on my financial level afford more rewarding vacations?" "How can I use my money to provide a generally more satisfying life?"

The answer is choice: setting priorities, consciously allocating resources for defined purposes. Unfortunately, setting financial priorities is extremely difficult. The normal difficulties in choosing between *any* alternatives are compounded by the alluring and endless options of our consumer society.

Fulfilling choices can be made, however. If you are frequently troubled by money questions, this chapter provides a framework for designing a financial master plan that will offer you or your family the greatest satisfaction. Working through the "Financial Planning Guide" that follows is an interesting and useful exercise that helps you live more comfortably within your income by forcing you to decide what's important to you. Your choices may seem strange or idiosyncratic to someone else, but acknowledging and respecting these personal values is at the heart of a truly workable financial plan.

In figuring your financial master plan, it will be helpful to have a pocket calculator designed for simple mathematical functions. A more complicated one won't be necessary.

Financial Planning Guide

Write down the household's *yearly* income—either net income ("take-home pay") if it comes from wages or salary only, or gross income if there are sources other than salary. On the same sheet of paper list your various expenses:

1. Fixed expenses. Money paid in fixed amounts. These expenses include:
   Debt repayments (bank loans, installment purchases)
   Insurance premiums
   Rent or mortgage payments
   Taxes (This applies only if your taxes are not withheld, or if you pay nonincome taxes such as property taxes.)

2. Flexible expenses. Expenses over which you have more control. Food, for instance, is necessary, but there is considerable leeway as to expenditure. This is also true of utilities. The most common flexible expenses include:

Automobile
Charitable contributions
Clothing
Entertainment
Food
Household (furniture, appliances, repairs, etc.)
Investments
Personal allowances
Savings
Schooling
Travel
Utilities

These aren't all the possible categories. A few other possibilities are: books and records, gifts, medical and dental (not covered by insurance), hobby or sports equipment. Keep the categories fairly broad. Thus, for example, include cosmetics under "clothing," and household supplies—detergent, cleansing powders, paper towels—under "food."

As an example, let's follow the master plan of a "typical" American family, John and Mary Michaels, and their little boy Jimmy. John, an assistant bank manager, grosses $23,500 per year, and Mary, an assistant buyer in a department store, earns $10,000. Their combined "take-home" income after withholding is $24,210.

Fixed expenses

First, John and Mary list the amounts paid out per year on their fixed expenses. These figures are listed on the next page.

Debts—$140 per month for the car ($3000 plus interest over 24 months)	$1680	per year
Insurance premiums—Life, home, fire, etc. (Health insurance is paid by their employers)	$1000	per year
Mortgage—$450 per month	$5400	per year
Taxes—a property tax of $500 per year *	$ 500	per year
Total fixed expenses	$8580	per year

They subtract $8580 from $24,210—deducting the fixed expenses from their take-home total—leaving a balance of $15,630 for flexible expenses.

Flexible expenses

Stage 1—Making Estimates

Now the fun begins. From the list of flexible expenses, John and Mary choose the categories they feel strongly about—the categories that rank #1 in *importance to them*. They put a "#1" next to each of these categories, and figure out, in rough accord with their actual income limitation, how much money they would like to spend on these items. Rough accord is necessary; you can't put down $5000 for household expenditures when disposable income is $8000. But you can let your imagination roam a little.

Going down the list alphabetically, Mary claims clothing as a #1 expense for her. She enjoys clothes, and her job as a buyer demands that she present a good appearance. $2000 seems a fair figure for her clothing budget. John, on

---

* John and Mary are both wage earners whose income taxes are withheld, so they don't have to put money aside for that. People who pay taxes directly should obtain the tax figures from their quarterly estimate and add 5% more for inflation.

the other hand, isn't interested in clothes; one suit per year plus various accessories is sufficient, so his clothes allocation is $500. Jimmy is 7 years old and growing rapidly, so John and Mary agree that $600 is about right for his clothes. Their total clothes budget is $3100.

Schooling is next. Jimmy is exceptionally intelligent, and teachers have recommended that he be sent to a private school for gifted children. John and Mary agree that Jimmy should have this opportunity, so they claim the $1100 yearly tuition as a #1 expense.

John claims occasional travel as a #1 item for himself. He finds that a change of scene relieves the tensions of his busy job. The Michaels family had in the past taken one family vacation per year in the car, and then John would average two short trips on his own. They agree to allot $2,000 for total family travel.

The #2 choices are considered next; that is, the categories that the family would *like* to spend money on, but do not feel as intensely about. For John and Mary, the first #2 choice is charitable contributions, so they agree to allocate $1,000 for that category. Entertainment is the next #2 category. Not only do John and Mary enjoy going out and entertaining, but John feels that party giving is an important source of business contacts. They figure that two good-sized parties per year, costing about $300 each (and partly tax deductible), plus frequent guests for cocktails, adds up to about $900. In addition, they both enjoy movies, theater, and ballet. An entertainment total of $1500 is allotted.

Household expenses are next on the #2 list. Although the Michaels anticipate no purchase of major appliances in the coming year, Mary thinks the living room could use some brightening and John is eager to fix up his workroom. They agree to keep these costs within $1100. Adding on another $1200 for repairs and unexpected expenses leaves a "household" total of $2300.

For John, personal allowance is a #2 category. He feels uncomfortable carrying less than $50, so his personal allowance is set at $75 per week, giving a year's total of $3900. Mary feels less strongly about a personal allowance, so she tables that item until they reach category #3.

Finally John and Mary face the remaining categories, all of which are #3 in rank. #3 categories may be crucial; everyone has to eat, and for many people an automobile is almost as essential. But the determining factor, however, is how much you *care*, beyond actual need.

The first #3 item on the Michaels' list is "automobile." For John and Mary a car is simply a means of transportation. Their car is not new—it had needed about $210 worth of servicing in the past year—but they feel it is sufficient for John's daily commute of twenty-five miles. A $680 allotment for gas and servicing (car insurance is covered under "premiums" in the "fixed expenses" list) seems sufficient.

Food doesn't present too much of a problem since the Michaels like simple meals, so they decide to keep within their present range of $75 per week for the family, which totals $3900 a year.

They decide to lump investments together with savings. (In a more elaborate financial planning setup, savings and investments might be considered separately, since they have somewhat different purposes.) John and Mary feel fairly secure—there is adequate insurance, they are each enrolled in pension plans at their jobs, and they have several thousand dollars in the bank. They realize that in a few years they will have to start saving intensively for Jimmy's college tuition and their own future, but they can coast along for now at their present savings rate of $100 per month, or $1200 per year.

Mary's personal allowance, which had been bypassed before, is set at $40 per week, from which she buys lunch at the low-cost employee dining room where she works, and contributes $5 per week to a car pool. The yearly sum adds up to $2080.

And last, utilities—the item least "interesting" to them—average $115 per month (including telephone, electricity, gas, water), totaling $1380.

Their flexible expenses are listed below.

#3	Automobile	$	680
#2	Charitable contributions		1000
#1	Clothing		3100
#2	Entertainment		1500
#3	Food		3900
#2	Household expenses (furniture, appliances, etc.)		2300
#3	Savings/investments		1200
#2	Personal allowance (John)		3900
#3	Personal allowance (Mary)		2080
#1	Schooling for Jimmy		1100
#1	Travel		2000
#3	Utilities		1380
			$24,140

"Lord, that's awful" John said to Mary, stunned, "since our disposable income is only $15,630; a difference of $8,510."

Mary was more sanguine. "I think it's important. It lets us know, first, the financial level we're aspiring to and secondly, it makes us evaluate the things that are really important. Let's try and work with this to bring it into line with our actual income, while still leaving money available for the things that matter most to us."

Stage 2—Cutting Costs

The Michaels' next step is to go through the #3 categories, and wherever possible, subtract a solid third from each allocation—and *then* decide how to make that cut tolerable. A one-third cut is hefty, but it makes sense as a substantial but not impossible reduction. Occasionally the estimate does have to be revised back upward, but surprisingly often the cut is manageable.

Automobile. They begin by reducing their original estimate of $680 by one-third to $454. The $680 had been based on the idea that John commutes 25 miles each day, using approximately 12 gallons of gas per week which, at 60¢ per gallon, totals about $375 per year. They estimated an additional $95 for general family driving (three gallons per week). The remaining $210 was for servicing. John now decides to join his colleagues in a round robin car pool; he will drive the car every third week, reducing his commutation bill to $125. Since the car won't be driven as often, $50 can be shaved from the servicing allotment, leaving a $160 balance. Thus, the total automobile allotment ends up at $380—even less than the original one-third cut.

Food. Lowering the food allocation from $3900 to $2600—a cut of $1300—seems a very big reduction indeed. Dividing the reduction by week results in a more manageable $25, leaving a total weekly food expenditure of $50. Surely, the Michaels think, that is possible. They agree to explore a variety of avenues: buying less expensive foods; buying and freezing supermarket specials in large quantities; canning and preserving at home; investigating creative economies like buying in bulk directly from wholesale sources; joining a food co-op; and/or growing some portion of food in a home garden. These economies can save quite a lot of money, but they are time-consuming. They virtually eliminate convenience foods and the quick steak for dinner, so one benefit must be weighed against the other. (See Chapter 15, page 218, for streamlined methods of meal planning and food preparation.)

Savings/investments. John and Mary agree that saving less than $100 per month is a mistake, so they decide to keep the present $1200.

Personal allowance (Mary). Cutting Mary's weekly pocket money from $40 to $27, a flat ⅓ reduction, seems too stringent, so she and John decide on $35, making that yearly allocation $1820.

Utilities. The original utilities estimate of $1380 had been based on their present rate of $115 per month—for electricity, gas, water, and a whopping average telephone bill of $40. John and Mary both use electricity carefully, and they agree to be even more observant of power-saving tips. Such small economies might reduce the electric bill to $68 per month.

The real problem, however, is the $40 phone bill. Mary makes long distance calls totaling $15 each month to her sister, Louise. But when John suggests curtailing the calls or writing letters, Mary gets upset. The calls turn out to be a higher priority than anticipated. They consider asking Louise to share the cost, but since she calls Mary about as often, her bill is probably about the same. So they agree to leave the long distance calls intact, and lower the remaining $25 per month by timing local calls to five minutes each, reducing the monthly bill to $35. So the utility allotment drops to only $1236 instead of the hoped-for $920, but there was a hidden priority that had to be taken into account.

John and Mary follow the same procedures for the #2 choices, this time, however, subtracting only ¼ instead of ⅓, since these are more important categories which demand more leeway.

Charitable contributions. Mary decides that since she spends hours working for her favorite charities and contrib-

utes clothes and appliances to the charity thrift shops (for a
tax deduction as well!), they can cut back on the cash contributions for the time being. The charity allotment is reduced from $1000 to $750.

Entertainment. The ¼ cut from $1500 reduces the en-
tertainment allotment by $375, to $1125. John and Mary
had originally planned on two parties during the year, but
decide that one party will be sufficient. They will save the
remaining $75 by getting cheaper theater seats and cutting
back a little.

Household expenses. In order to reduce the household
allocation by ¼, from $2300 to $1725, the Michaels cut the
household "reserve" fund from $1200 to $1000. They decide to do some of the work themselves, and Mary will arrange for a seamstress friend to make slipcovers in exchange for Mary's fashion counseling. They will postpone
buying the less important living room items until next
year.

Personal allowance (John). John admits that he might
not need $75 pocket money per week, so a compromise sum
of $60 is agreed upon, reducing that allotment to $3120.

For the #1 categories, it's best to be creative and flexible rather than set a firm reduction figure.

Clothing. John feels he can reduce his clothing allotment from $500 to $350. Jimmy's is also reduced from $600
to $350. How many pairs of blue jeans and sneakers can one
little boy wear? Mary is more of a problem since this is a
high priority for her. She lowers her clothes budget to
$1,000 by careful wardrobe planning plus creative shop-
ping: in addition to shopping at a discount in the department store where she works, she will explore unconven-

tional outlets like resale shops, discount houses, and manufacturers' outlets. The Michaels' clothing allotment is now reduced to $1700.

Schooling for Jimmy. This is a fixed tuition fee of $1100, but John and Mary reserve the option to try for a scholarship or a loan.

Travel. Touring in the car is a relatively inexpensive form of family travel, but John enjoys an occasional short trip alone. If the family goes backpacking and canoeing— costing no more than $400—John can take one lavish three-day trip for $750, and another $350 excursion, thus cutting travel from $2000 to $1500.

The first round of budget cuts over, the Michaels' draw up a new list.

#3	Automobile	$ 380
#2	Charitable contributions	750
#1	Clothing	1700
#2	Entertainment	1125
#3	Food	2600
#2	Household expenses (furniture, appliances, etc.)	1725
#3	Savings/investments	1200
#2	Personal allowance (J)	3120
#3	Personal allowance (M)	1820
#1	Jimmy's schooling	1100
#1	Travel	1500
#3	Utilities	1236
		$18,256

They are now only $2626 over the flexible income total of $15,630—a lot more manageable than the original $8,510 discrepancy, but necessitating another round of cutting.

Stage 3—To the Bone

Automobile. No reduction is possible in this category.

Charitable contributions. Reluctantly the Michaels lower their charity allocation to a rock bottom of $250.

Clothing. Mary's $1000 allocation still seems too high; she can manage with $750. Both John and Jimmy make small reductions, bringing the total Smith clothing budget down to $1350.

Entertainment. John and Mary agree to hold firm at $1125.

Food. Their reduction to $2600 seems the bare minimum.

Household expenses. A reduction to $1500.

Savings/investments. No reduction possible.

Personal allowance (John). John agrees to $50 per week, bringing his personal allotment to $2600.

Personal allowance (Mary). $1040.

Schooling for Jimmy. $1100.

Travel. This item, because it means so much to John to go away a couple of times a year, takes some discussion. Since travel means very little to Mary, the Michaels decide to forego a family vacation this year; Jimmy can attend a summer day camp that costs $150. John, however, will still take his two trips, one for $200 and one for $750. This leaves a travel allotment of $1100.

Utilities. $1236.

The Michaels' list now reflects their latest cuts. Their budget is now only $631 away from the disposable income limit of $15,630! So John and Mary decide to take a personal loan for Jimmy's schooling: $1100 at 18% interest over 36 months works out to $432.60 per year. Their yearly expenditures are now set at $15,594—$36 less than the

Automobile	$ 380
Charitable contributions	250
Clothing	1350
Entertainment	1125
Food	2600
Household expenses (furniture, appliances, etc.)	1500
Savings/investments	1200
Personal allowance (John)	2600
Personal allowance (Mary)	1820
Schooling for Jimmy	1100
Travel	1100
Utilities	1236
	$16,261

$15,630 goal. So John and Mary have designed their master plan, with even a bit of money left over.

As you design your own plan, keep in mind that John's and Mary's decisions and compromises might not be right for you. You might not even approve of them! John may seem self-indulgent insisting on those private trips, but he has been flexible in every other area precisely so that he may have relative mobility on this, to him, important point.

No matter how illogical your priority may seem to someone else, you have a right to it—as long as you're prepared to compromise or even be severely restricted in other areas to compensate for relative freedom in a priority.

With that in mind, here is brief summary of the financial planning procedure.

Summary of the Financial Planning Guide

1. Note the household's yearly income—either net ("take-home pay") if all income derives from wages or salary, or gross if from other sources.

2. List all your expenses under two major headings, "fixed expenses" and "flexible expenses."

3. Add up the amounts paid out yearly under the "fixed expenses" category, and subtract from the yearly income. This leaves a balance to be allocated among the flexible expenses.

4. Go down the "flexible" list and select the categories that the various members of the household feel most strongly about. Mark these #1, and figure out, in rough accord with your actual income limitation, how much money you would like to allocate to each of these.

5. Select the #2 categories and figure out money allocations for these categories.

6. Do the same with #3 categories.

7. Add up all the "flexible expenses." If they total a sum no more than the disposable income as noted in Step 3, congratulations. You are living within your income. If the total sum is more than your disposable income, go on to the next step.

8. Consider each #3 category in turn as follows:

    a. Subtract ⅓ of the present allocation. If, for example, a #3 allocation is $900, revise it down to $600.

    b. Consider how that item might be pared down to fit within the reduced limit. See pages 93–95 to familiarize yourself with some of the kinds of thinking involved.

9. Consider each #2 item in turn as follows:

    a. Subtract ¼ of the present alloation. If, for example, a #2 allocation is $1,000, revise it down to $750.

    b. Consider how that item might be pared down to fit within the reduced limit. See pages 95–96 for pointers.

10. Consider each #1 item as follows: Don't make an absolute cut; rather, consider how your needs might be met within a less expansive financial framework. See pages 96–97 for some of the ideas involved.

11. Add up and total the revised #1, #2, and #3 figures. If you are now within your disposable income range (the balance arrived at in Step 3), excellent. Your work is done. If not:

12. Go through the list again, paring down as much as you can—*but* never lose sight of your priorities. Try to keep your #1 selections as generous as you can because they are most important to you. See pages 98–99 for some approaches to this process. Keep at this until expenses have been brought into line with income.

By now you have established a basic financial planning framework that will function effectively for a long time. I recommend that you adjust it yearly—probably at tax time, while your financial situation is still fresh in your mind—to take into consideration increase or decrease in income, completion of installment debts, a change in priorities. As the needs of living change, so does the budget.

7
The Mechanics of Money

Many people are intimidated by the mechanics of handling money. One of my clients was always mislaying her bills, never knew the amount of her bank balance, and lived with the threat that her electricity might be turned off at any moment. Finally she concocted a system born of desperation: she sent off $50 every so often to the electric company in the hope that this amount would cover her bill. We devised an easier and more reliable system for her, and you can do the same for yourself. A few hours one day per month will generally be sufficient to take care of all money transactions.

Setting Up the System

If you designed a master plan similar to the one described in Chapter 5, draw up a monthly chart in order to keep actual expenses within the plan's guidelines. Again, we'll use John and Mary Michaels as the example:

1. Divide each yearly allocation by 12 months and round off. The Michaels' breakdown is shown below.

Expenses	*Yearly*	*Monthly*
Automobile	$ 380	$ 32
Charitable contributions	250	21
Clothing	1350	113
Entertainment	1125	94
Food	2600	217
Household expenses	1500	125
(furniture, appliances, etc.)		
Savings/investments	1200	100
Personal allowance (John)	2600	217
Personal allowance (Mary)	1820	152
Jimmy's schooling (loan)	433	36
Travel	1100	92
Utilities	1236	103
Total	$15,594	$1302

2. List the categories of your *flexible* expenses on a Discretionary Chart. *This step is only for those who are using a master plan,* and is a handy way to keep track of your flexible expenses on a month-to-month basis. Take a single month's allocation—say, for car expenses,

Figure 2 The Michaels' discretionary chart of flexible Expenses (*facing page*)

	Jan.	Feb.	Mar.	Apr.	May	June	July	Aug.	Sept.	Oct.	Nov.	Dec.
Car Expenses	32	64	96	128	160	192	224	256	288	320	352	384
Charity	21	42	63	84	105	126	147	168	189	210	231	252
Clothes	113	256	339	452	565	678	791	904	1017	1130	1243	1356
Entertainment	94	188	282	376	470	564	658	752	846	940	1034	1128
Food	217	434	651	868	1085	1302	1519	1736	1953	2170	2387	2604
Household	125	250	375	500	625	750	875	1000	1125	1250	1375	1500
Travel	92	184	276	368	460	552	644	736	828	920	1012	1104
Utilities	103	206	309	412	515	618	721	824	927	1030	1133	1236

	Jan.	Feb.	Mar.	Apr.	May	June	July	Aug.	Sept.	Oct.	Nov.	Dec.
Car payments ($140)												
School loan ($36)												
Mortgage ($450)												
Savings ($100)												
John's allowance ($217)												
Mary's allowance ($152)												
Taxes ($42-$125 quarterly)	✱			✱		✱			✱			
Insurance* ($42-$125 quarterly)	✱			✱			✱			✱		

* Make a separate box for each type of insurance you have—health, life, etc.

$32—and enter that in the top half of the January box, leaving the bottom half blank. Add $32 to the first $32, making $64 for the upper half of the February box. Another $32 for March makes $96, and on through the year. Use a pocket calculator for the arithmetic.

Write the estimated monthly totals in red, to distinguish them from the actual expenses that will eventually be filled in on the bottom half.

The Michaels' chart is shown in Figure 2.

3. *Whether or not you have a master plan,* draw up another chart of fixed monthly or quarterly expenses. (See Figure 3.) This chart consists of any item that recurs in a fixed amount on a regular basis, such as debt or installment payments, regular sums allocated to savings, rent or mortgage payments, taxes, and insurance premiums.

The asterisks in the "Taxes" and "Insurance" columns signify the months that quarterly payments are due. The IRS dates are the same for everyone. The insurance dates will depend, of course, on your own policies. Use of this chart will be discussed later in the chapter.

Banking

I recommend a minimum of three bank accounts:

1. *Savings.* If you're married, your savings account should be a joint one. If one partner is incapacitated, the other has immediate access to the money; if the account is in one name only, legal problems will arise.

2. *Checking.* You should have one checking account that is used only once a month for paying bills. For couples, open a joint account so either party can write the checks.

Figure 3 The Michaels' fixed expenses chart (*facing page*)

Although one person will generally handle the finances (see page 109), the other partner should be in a position to pay the bills if circumstances call for that.

Consider whether to opt for "special" checking or "regular" checking. No minimum balance is required for special checking, but the bank charges 10¢ or 15¢ per check, plus a monthly maintenance fee. A regular checking account is free, but you must always keep a minimum balance in the account, usually $300 or $500.

Some large corporations make special arrangements with nearby banks to offer their employees free checking.

3. *Checking.* Each person should have his or her own personal checking account for ordinary cash expenses. Deposit your personal allowance in this account. For couples, one person should be designated "food buyer," and the monthly food allotment should go into that person's account. Paying expenses by check helps you keep track of where the money is going.

The bank you choose to give your business to will, in most cases, simply be the one that's most convenient. If, however, you have some equidistant alternatives, select the bank that offers services and a friendly attitude. Services include:

Interbranch check-cashing.

Machine check-cashing.

Cash-reserve or checking-plus checking. (There are in effect personal loans.)

Night deposits.

Special services—safety deposit boxes, traveler's checks, exchange of foreign currency, credit cards (some banks have a service charge, others don't), estate planning. Ask about other services.

Substantial gifts for substantial new account deposits.

Sometimes a small neighborhood branch may offer more advantages than a large midtown bank. Since you become acquainted with the staff, you may feel freer about asking for help in a crisis, such as an emergency overdraft. A small-branch officer is also somewhat more willing to spend time when a modest sum of money is involved, to advise you in financial planning and taking advantage of special services the bank may offer. He or she may also be more helpful in granting you a personal loan.

A savings bank offers savings accounts at a somewhat higher rate of interest than a commercial bank, and many now offer free checking accounts for depositors. However, they don't generally have as wide a range of services as do commercial banks. Their traditional function is to offer mortgage loans for buying or building homes.

Before dealing with any bank, check to see that it has been insured by the Federal Deposit Insurance Corporation (FDIC) or the Federal Savings & Loan Insurance Corporation (FSLIC), both of which insure your deposits up to a specified amount.

The Monthly Procedure

This procedure applies to everyone, whether or not you've designed a master plan. Choose one person in the household to regularly act as "financier"—to deposit checks in the bill-paying account and pay the bills. Then select a firm date on or near the first of each month or near the monthly arrival of your bank statement, and balance your check-book and pay the bills on that date. Hold any bill that arrives later until the accounting date of the next month. If you feel the entire procedure of reconciling checkbooks and paying bills is too much for one day's work, reconcile bank statements a day or two *before* the bill-paying day; that too should be a regular appointment. Follow this monthly procedure:

1. Assemble equipment and supplies, which are:
   a. Financial folder with pocket. This is the financial folder discussed in Chapter 5, page 68. As bills, bank statements, bank deposit slips, investment notices, anything to do with money, come in during the month, put them in the folder. Don't try to act on them until your monthly appointment unless there is an emergency of some kind.
   b. Sales slips. Make sure you have sales slips for all charge purchases, and save them. If you charge groceries, a kitchen drawer is a good place to keep grocery slips. A dresser drawer might be used for slips involving clothing purchases. Or put the slips directly into the financial folder if that is convenient. When you begin moneywork, collect all the slips and put them with the financial folder.
   c. Discretionary Chart and chart of expenses. Keep these permanently in the financial folder.
   d. Payment booklets for bank loans and car installments. Keep them in the financial folder.
   e. Calculator.
   f. Checkbook for bill-paying account. Keep it permanently in or near the financial folder.
   g. Blank envelopes and stamps.

2. Sorting out. Divide the contents of the financial folder into five piles:
   a. Banking: statements, cancelled checks, deposit slips, and any other bank notices.
   b. Bills, notices of renewals (magazines, club dues, and so forth), any correspondence that will require payment by check.
   c. Payment booklets for debts (bank loans, installment payments) or other fixed obligations.
   d. All sales slips and cash register slips.
   e. Anything else, such as investment notices.

3. Reconcile the bank statements. In honesty, there's a fair chance that life would run smoothly if you never reconciled a bank statement. But banks do make mistakes. A client once had $500,000 accidentally *credited* to his account! The bank caught that one soon enough. If you've not been reconciling up till now, the reconciling instructions on the bank statement or envelope, although adequate for someone already familiar with the task, don't give enough detail for a novice. A bank officer might be willing to start you off in the right direction. But if you're on your own, forget the past and start with the most recent statement: *

   a. Put the cancelled checks in numerical order. There will probably be numerical gaps, representing checks that have not yet been cashed. The bank statement itself should also be in front of you.

   b. Note the sum on the top check—the amount only, not the payee—and look through the statement listing until you find that sum. (Note: Some banks themselves now list the checks in numerical order.) Cross the sum off the statement and go on until you've finished the pile of checks.

   c. If you have a special checking account, two additional amounts will be listed on your statement: check charges plus a monthly maintenance fee. Add these, subtract the total from your checkbook balance, and cross them off the statement. Remaining amounts on the statement would be one of the following:

   A penalty for a bounced check, or a special charge, such as for new checkbooks. In either case, the bank will have sent you an "advice." Cross that sum off the statement and subtract it from your checkbook balance.

   A mistake caused by skipping a check as you flipped

---

* If you itemize income tax deductions, keep cancelled checks for a period of seven years. You can throw away older checks. If you don't itemize, keep checks for one year and discard older ones.

quickly through the pile. Make sure that no two checks are stuck together.

The bank may have charged someone else's check to your account. We'll get to that later.

d. Now reconcile the cancelled checks against your own record in your checkbook. Beginning, for example, with #801, mark the 801 stub entry. Continue this way for all the cancelled checks. When you come to a gap—#811 is missing—don't mark off 811 in your checkbook. The check hasn't cleared yet, and it will probably appear on next month's statement. Also mark off the subtractions you just made for service charge and any penalties.

e. Select the deposit slips that register on this month's statement and mark them off in your checkbook as you did with the checks. *Don't check off deposits not registered on the bank statement*. Put the registered deposit slips with the cancelled checks.

f. Figure out your current balance by following the instructions on the form imprinted either on the reverse side of the statement or on the envelope. Here's a brief summary:

List all outstanding checks—that is, checks that have not cleared and are not checked off in your checkbook, and add them up.

Add up the deposit slips that did *not* appear on this month's statement, plus your balance on the closing day of the statement (that balance is printed on the front of the statement).

Subtract the total amount of checks outstanding from the sum you arrived at in the preceding step.

The remainder should conform to your checkbook balance. If there's a small discrepancy, up to about $10, you can generally assume that the bank's computers are accurate, and you have made an error on your check stubs. Correct your checkbook balance accordingly and don't worry about it. If there's a significant discrepancy, recheck your addition and subtraction carefully. The mistake probably lies in that area.

g. Follow-up. At this point you would ordinarily close the books until next month, but some situations require follow-up action:

If there is a significant discrepancy between your balance and the bank's, take your materials to the bank and have them work out the problem.

If there is an unresolved sum listed in the bank statement, take statement and cancelled checks to the bank.

If a check hasn't cleared by the time you have received two bank statements, get in touch with the payee to see if it has been put through. In many localities, a check is no longer valid thirty days after its date.

If a deposit slip has not appeared on two statements, take slip and statements to the bank.

h. When everything is reconciled, put the statement, cancelled checks, deposit slips, and advices into the statement envelope, write the month and year on the outside, and put it into a drawer or small accordion file. The deposit slips that were not covered in this month's statement should be put back in the financial folder for next month. Note: If you itemize income tax deductions, you might want to organize your checks at this point, or you may choose not to. See page 115 for a discussion of handling tax materials.

4. Now turn to the payment of bills. Check the sales slips for department store and credit card purchases against the itemization on the bill, and staple the slips to the bill stub that you keep. Write a check for each bill (always fill in the stub—it is important for reconciling and for taxes).

5. Collect all sales slips and bill stubs—the part that you retain for yourself—put them into an envelope, write

the month and year on the outside, and put the envelope with the bank statement.

6. Investments in stocks and bonds generate stock transaction notices and other kinds of paper. You will get buying and selling notices from your broker for each transaction, plus a monthly stock summary that should be checked so that it conforms to the individual slips. At the end of the year there is a notice summarizing dividends received. All these materials should be saved for the purposes of computing capital gains taxes.

7. Fixed obligations. Take Chart #2 (see page 106) and your payment booklets. Write checks for all items listed (loans, installment payments, savings deposits, personal allowances, etc.) and check the appropriate box. If it is *not* a payment month for quarterly taxes, put a dash in the box. If it *is* a payment month, write out your check and mark the appropriate box. Handle the quarterly insurance payments the same way.

8. Filing. The simplest way to file the bill stubs and bank statements is in an accordion folder by month. Some people who itemize income tax deductions prefer, however, to sort them into their deduction categories—charitable contributions, medical expenses, interest (the finance charge on revolving charge accounts is counted as interest), business expenses—at this time. The nondeductible bills and checks would then just be filed by month. This is all right, but I personally prefer to sort these items out in one yearly work session.

   Some people "overfile" by making separate filing sections for say, electric company, each department store, telephone company, etc. In most cases this adds an unnecessary precision to the money-handling procedure.

9. If you don't itemize income taxes, glance through the bills from one year ago this month to see whether there is a bill for a major purchase that you might want to keep permanently; if so, file it in the regular filing system under "Household" or "Warranties" if it's an appliance, or under "Art" if it's a painting or photograph. Throw away the remainder of the bills. If you do itemize, keep last year's bills untiĪ you prepare your taxes.

10. If you use the master plan, read page 116.

Summary of Financial Handling Checklist

This summary briefly restates the principles and procedures involved in carrying through a monthly moneywork enterprise.

1. Select a monthly date for handling all financial obligations.
2. Assemble equipment and supplies.
3. Sort all materials in the financial folder into five piles:
   a. Banking materials.
   b. Bills to pay.
   c. Payment booklets for fixed obligations.
   d. All sales slips and cash register slips.
   e. Anything else, such as investment notices.
4. Reconcile the bank statements with your checkbooks. Put the completed statements in a desk drawer or file.
5. Write checks for the bills, put *your* portions of the bills to one side.
6. Collect all bill stubs and sales slips in an envelope, mark it with the month and year, and put it in the same drawer or file as the bank statements.
7. Check stock transaction notices.

8. Write checks for the fixed obligations (Chart #2), and check off the chart.
9. If you don't itemize income taxes, throw out the bill stubs and cancelled checks from one year ago. If you do itemize, hold for tax work.
10. If you use the master plan, calculate those allocations.

Incorporating the Master Plan

To put your master plan to practical use you'll need the Discretionary Chart (see page 105), your carry-around notebook, calculator, personal checkbook (not the bill-paying account), and all bills and sales slips. Proceed as follows:

1. Head a page in the notebook with each category on the Discretionary Chart.
2. Take a department store bill with sales slips attached. Say, in one case, there are three sales slips—for a skirt and sweater set, a sports jacket, and a chess set. Note the skirt and sweater sum on the "clothing" page (just the amount—no other information needed), and also the sports jacket. If there's more than one person buying clothes, add that person's initial as well. The chess set is more flexible—it might go on the "hobby" page or under "entertainment" or "gifts"; whichever category can best afford it. There will always be minor adjustments for expenses that don't fit clearly into one category. Follow the same procedure for the rest of the department store bills and the credit cards.
3. Do the same with all other bills. Mark the electric and phone bills under "utilities"; a magazine renewal might be "books" or "hobby" or "entertainment." A doctor bill would obviously be "medical," and a plumber's bill is "household."

4. Enter all remaining sales slips and cash register slips on the appropriate category page. Also check the stubs in your *personal* checkbook (not the bill-paying checkbook). Cash expenses—a movie, for instance, is "entertainment"—should be marked in the book as you go along.

5. Add up the figures on each of the category pages. The same page can be used month after month until you fill it up, so long as you cross off the previous months to avoid confusion. This is just for figuring, it is not a permanent record.

6. Using your Discretionary Chart (see page 105) fill in the bottom half with the actual amount spent for the month, added up from your notebook list. The top figure in each box is the sum that *should* have been spent up to that point according to the master plan allocation. The two amounts—the ideal and the actual—will not always match. Clothes buying, for example, is usually concentrated in spring and fall, so the actual expenditure through July may not come up to the "guideline" amount—but will be made up in August or September. Similarly, food buying in bulk may mean very heavy expenditures one month and light ones the next.

   The allocated amounts in the Discretionary Chart are guidelines that you adjust continually. For example, if actual entertainment expenditures through June are $620, while the chart says $564, don't despair. Go easy on evenings out, and adjust entertainment expenditures on the chart by September. As long as you know what your course *is*, you can diverge from it a bit to explore interesting byways—and come back again.

7. When an installment debt is completed, or if there is an increase or decrease in income, revise the master plan to incorporate the new situation.

PART FOUR

The Home

8

Storage Basics: Where Things Go

We all have a tendency to accumulate clothes, games, papers, photos, toys, tools, and other objects of twentieth-century life, but when accumulation turns from minor idiosyncracy into anarchy, the reorganization of living and storage space becomes a top priority. This chapter tackles the basics of clearing out and organizing general-use closets, cabinets, and other storage areas, and offers tips on how to create new storage places, and how to be sure that you can find everything again. (Clothes closets and accessories are discussed separately in Chapter 9, page 143–147.)

The chapter is planned so that you can work at a pace of one or two hours at a time. This is important. Set a definite regular time for closet work for the next several weeks, and write down the date in your appointment calendar. It could be an hour a day, or an hour twice a week—whatever you can spare. And, most important of all, when the hour is up, *quit!* You won't become frustrated, and the closets will get organized.

Organizing Closets

Stage 1: Targeting a closet

Is there a particular category of object you've been itching to organize—toys, vases and decorative ware, carpentry tools? If so, your starting point is to pinpoint a particular cabinet or closet that would be the most convenient place to house these objects, preferably near to where they are used. For instance, is the proposed toy cabinet in or near the children's playroom? Is the photographic equipment cabinet accessible to the darkroom? Does the closet contain shelves and/or hooks of the kind you will need? You can always modify a closet, but your task will be simpler if the closet is already designed to meet your storage needs. Don't try to assemble whatever object you've chosen to organize at this early stage, just pick an appropriate location.

On the other hand, a particular *closet* may be the trouble spot. If so, *that's* your "target closet" and that's where you begin. Choose its function, if one is not already established, by asking yourself, "People pass this closet on their way to where?" A cabinet between kitchen and dining room, presently cluttered with luggage, old photographs, games, and offseason clothes, could be used for kitchen overflow and serving pieces. Similarly, a closet between bedrooms would make a natural linen closet. This is a principle:

Principle #6   **Store things at or near the point where they are used.**

If you feel too overwhelmed to choose a target closet, the best solution is to—literally—flip a coin or stand in the center of a room, close your eyes, and point. Decide on that closet's function. Your target closet may eventually house a variety of objects, but you are determining its primary function at this point.

Stage 2: Weeding out

Have on hand a good supply of grocery cartons. Mark one box "throwaway" and one "giveaway" and weed out the target closet. The process is to consider each item individually and ask yourself:

1. Have I used this article in the past year? If not,
2. Does it have value to me, sentimental or monetary? If the answer is no but you're still not sure whether to keep it or not, ask the clincher:
3. Might it come in handy someday?

When the answer to the third question is yes, put the article into the "throwaway" or "giveaway" box. That phrase almost always indicates that you are hanging on to clutter.

Work on one small section at a time. *Do not* under any circumstances empty the whole target closet at once. This warning is crucial. The resulting chaos is sure to set you back or even put you off completely. Instead, concentrate today for an hour or two on the two lower left-hand shelves. Tomorrow tackle the other two left shelves, then the two right lower shelves the day after, and so forth. During the sometimes painful process of throwing things away, it helps to invite a friend or relative to keep you company and prevent you from vacillating over your decisions to keep or not to keep. If, as sometimes happens, you find you want a replacement for a particular article that has been discarded, consider the money well spent in exchange for functional closets.

Place things that you intend to keep in the target closet into cartons labeled "target closet." Stack the other articles into roughly organized piles—piles of books, piles of clothes, piles of toys, etc.—or into cartons marked with the name of the category. Wrap breakables either in old sheets or towels, or in tissue wrap paper or newspaper.

Fifteen minutes before you stop closet work for the day, push the target-closet boxes back into the closet (simply to get them out of the way), and distribute as many of the remaining piles or cartons as you can near their eventual location. Slip books into any available bookshelves or pile them on the floor nearby, put papers into the office area for sorting, put clothes into another closet and toys and games in the children's room. Do not, however, try organizing *those* closets or shelves. You'll get to that later. For the objects whose eventual whereabouts is a mystery, choose an out-of-the-way corner and call it a storage catchall.

The point of roughly organizing and tidying up before finishing the day's closet work is twofold: your progress will become apparent, which will encourage you to complete the job; and each day's work will be completed with a sense of "wrap-up." Undoubtedly you will be living for a while with boxes or piles, but as long as they are orderly and in place, you won't be as easily discouraged.

Continue the weeding-out process day by day until the target closet is completely bare.

Stage 3: Assembling

Many of the articles destined for the target closet are probably stored in other closets, or piled in some corners of the house. Your next task is to root them out. In order not to disrupt the whole household, tackle the problem in this manner: starting in the room where the target closet is located, pull out from other closets or storage areas in that room any "target" articles. *Do not empty out or attempt to organize the closet you are pulling from!* Your treasure hunt should be limited to whatever target articles you can easily reach. Anything deeply buried that cannot be reached without pulling out the entire closet can stay buried until *that* closet is reorganized. Proceed to all closets and storage areas in that room, putting the target objects into cartons and culling giveaways and throwaways as you work. At the end of the work session, push the target cartons into the target closet.

Work systematically from room to room until you've covered all areas and have a clearly defined set of objects to be stored in the target closet.

Stage 4: Setting up the closet and keeping it that way

First consider whether the closet is structurally functional. Does it contain enough shelves and/or hanging space to house the articles? Might there be a need for supplemental storage spaces outside the closet proper? If existing space or facilities are significantly insufficient—"significantly" as opposed to the minor supplement of a few hooks or an additional shelf or two—turn to page 129, "If Only I Had More Space." Execute whatever improvements in or outside the closet you judge necessary. Then, before stocking the closet, you might want to clean, paint, line, or otherwise spruce it up.

The basic rule in stocking a closet is to keep frequently used objects low and accessible, to store items used less often on higher shelves or out of the way, and not to stack more than three pieces that are not a set on top of each other. It also helps in maintaining a storage system to keep items used together near one another; for example, ice bucket and bar equipment, or tennis racquet, balls, togs, sneakers, and admittance card to the tennis club.

If there's no light fixture in the closet, keep a flashlight tied to a hook so no one, including you, will "borrow" it.

Two techniques will help keep your closets streamlined: *immediately* assign a place for anything new that you buy. If you would like to switch it around later, fine; but it is courting disaster to leave an article "around" with a view to making a decision sometime later. Second, at the beginning of each season look over each closet and cabinet to identify items unused during the past season. Following the guidelines on page 123, discard any items that have outlived their usefulness.

The Coat Closet. To illustrate how to best utilize a closet without making structural changes and with only minor supplements, let's take the coat closet of an active family with young children. The coat closet is typically one of the most chaotic closets in the house because it houses a wide variety of objects and is so heavily used.

The first goal, especially with children, is to encourage everyone to put away his or her coats, hats, scarves, and gloves. The solution: make putting away so easy that a person has to go out of the way *not* to.

For scarves and hats, one family—husband, wife, and three children—installed five sturdy hooks on the back of the closet door in the pattern shown in Figure 4.

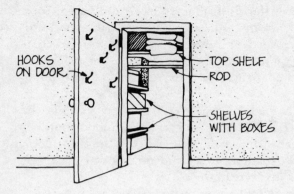

Figure 4 Efficient use of space in a family coat closet

The two smaller children hung scarf and hat on the lower hooks. The oldest child took the middle hook, and the two top hooks were assigned to the adults. Extra scarves and hats were stored on side shelves in special boxes made by cutting out one panel of a cardboard box—boot boxes are about the right size—to make a container whose contents are on display and easy to reach without disturbing the rest of the closet. If the closet door doesn't lend itself to hat and scarf hooks, put up a rack on the wall near the door—again, adjusted to the height of the smallest child. Alternatively, consider any convenient drawer or shelf in the vicinity: a sideboard with an empty drawer, a shelf in the nearby kitchen, a small chest of drawers near the closet.

Gloves can be stored in these drawers too, or tossed in a small basket placed on a side shelf of the closet or nailed to the wall. For children's winter mittens, string a clothesline with clothespins along the back of the closet door. Store extra gloves in the box with extra scarves and hats.

Hang adult coats, of course, on the closet rod. Put height-adjusted hooks inside the closet for young children.

A coat rack, either the old-fashioned freestanding kind or a handsome wall rack installed on a near wall, is a good supplement to the closet. It is more convenient for guests' coats than squeezing them into the closet. A single person or couple might use a coat rack for everything: coat, hat, handbag, briefcase.

An umbrella rack or stand near the door can also be useful. To hang out wet coats, lay a strip of indoor-outdoor carpeting underneath a wall rack right by the front door. Keep boots and overshoes in a handsome box or basket by the entrance, or in a box in the closet.

If the closet is still too crowded, select each person's most frequently worn coats and consign the rest to a bedroom or storage closet, or consider the suggestions on page 132 for adding new closet space.

Stage 5: New closets to conquer

Choose a new target closet and repeat the process already described. The only difference is that in Stage 4, the assembling stage, also check the storage catchall corner you established in Stage 3.

When you've finished all the closets, turn your attention to any miscellaneous piles or storage catchalls and house those objects in whatever free spaces may have been opened by the main reorganizing job. Relate minor categories, if possible, to the closet's major category. For example, the toy cabinet, even allowing for toy expansion, might contain other child-related objects: clothes that are still too large to wear, extra school supplies. Or, if the toy cabinet isn't in the children's bedroom, adult games might find their home there: playing cards, poker chips, Scrabble.

Closet Organizing Summary

1. Choose a closet to work on and assign it a function.
2. Empty the closet, weeding out throwaways and give-aways, and distributing other items appropriately.
3. Work systematically from room to room, closet to closet, assembling all articles that belong in the closet you are working on. Don't try to organize or rearrange the closet you're pulling *from*. Cull giveaways and throwaways as you go along.
4. Analyze whether the target closet requires major changes. If so, execute them, following guidelines in "If Only I Had More Space."
5. Spruce up the closet and stock it.
6. Go to the next closet and continue until all the closets and miscellaneous storage piles are organized.

"If Only I Had More Space"

In our homes, about eighty percent of overcrowding is a result of disorganized space rather than insufficient space. New or expanded storage units often only create more places to be disorganized in. So always *organize* existing storage space before trying to increase or change it. Once you've done that however, if your space is still insufficient or inappropriate for your chosen purposes, expand or modify the areas through the various techniques discussed here.

This section is a broadbased approach to storage in general. For storage techniques that apply to specific situations, see individual chapters.

Taking advantage of what you've got: ways of using space you haven't thought of

The hanging and shelving techniques discussed later in this chapter may provide a solution for you, but first consider "easy storage": spaces already functional that require little or no installation work. This is a principle:

Principle #7 **The less work any project costs you in terms of installation or general aggravation, the easier it will be achieved.**

Neither furniture nor any household object has to be used as the designer intended. Extra bookshelves can house a portable sewing machine or household supplies. Curtain the space if you'd like, or put up an attractive screen. Similarly, use decorative objects as storage containers. One client stored small household items—glue, lubricating oil, pliers, in an earthenware bowl placed just high enough so the objects remained hidden. Baskets of any size can hold a number of things. As a general rule of thumb when considering furniture and objects, *any hollow space is a potential container.* See Chapter 13, page 201, for additional furniture-as-storage ideas.

Consider also the storage potential of any space between objects. Can a folding stepladder fit in the small gap between washing machine and sink? What about a rack to hold newspapers or garbage bags? A small space between an open door and the wall behind it might accommodate a fold-up drying rack, ironing board, or folding chairs. The spaces underneath furniture are potential storage areas too. One client kept her knitting bag underneath the TV chair so she could knit whenever the impulse took her while watching television. In her case, the chair was skirted and hid the bag from view.

Consider making better use of corners. A decorative screen or hanging curtain might be drawn over a corner to hide caddies of cleaning supplies, games, boxes of offseason clothes, whatever seems appropriate. This is one example of the general principle of "divide and store." Any part of a room can be divided by screen or curtain to create a storage area—sometimes to attractive effect. One client whose living room was long and narrow changed its proportions, and made a new storeroom for himself, by hanging a floor-to-ceiling drape all the way across the room.

Another "easy storage" idea is to use the "organizers" that can be purchased in many variety stores. However, before you buy these, decide first how the organizer will be used; the organizers themselves won't organize you. There are a number of different kinds on the market for various purposes—vinyl storage cubes, plastic vegetable bins, wall organizers. Specific suggestions for their use will appear in later chapters.

If miscellaneous items are stored in a number of areas, you might list the locations and file the list in your "Household" folder so you can find something at a glance.

Expanding or modifying closet space

First assemble the articles that require storage (see "Assembling," page 125). When you know their size and quantity, whether it's a collection of small tools and household implements, or bulky items like extra bedding or luggage, you can choose intelligently between the two primary techniques for expanding or modifying storage space: shelving and hanging.

Shelves *

1. Line one or more sides of a clothes closet with shelves.
2. Convert a shallow clothes closet to a cabinet by building shelves from top to bottom. This won't work well in a deep closet because the back is too hard to reach unless the shelves pull out, a much more elaborate construction project.
3. If you are *extremely* handy, consider a floor-to-ceiling revolving lazy susan. This of course would work best in a deeper closet.
4. Convert a wide clothes closet into a dual purpose closet/cabinet by partitioning and building shelves in part of the closet.
5. Carefully measure the closet's dimensions and buy a freestanding cabinet, either open-shelved or fitted with drawers.
6. Make a storage unit from a wide, deep clothes closet by installing shelves, supported by posts, as in Figure 5.
7. Convert a cabinet into a clothes closet by removing the shelves and installing clothes racks. See Chapter 8 for details on clothes closets.
8. If your closet is high and has open space in its upper reaches, install shelves for luggage and seldom-used items.

Shelf Tips

1. When possible, install adjustable shelves.
2. Store items of approximately the same height on the same shelves. To set shelf height, measure a few typical items and allow a few inches above that.

---

* If you intend to do the work yourself, consult *Instant–Effect Decorating* by Marjorie P. Katz (paperback—Signet, 1973); *The Better Homes & Gardens Handyman's Book* (paperback—Bantam, 1974); *Okay, I'll Do It Myself: A Handy Woman's Primer* by Barbara Curry (paperback—Random House, 1971); or *The Reader's Digest Complete Do-It-Yourself* (Reader's Digest/Norton, 1973.)

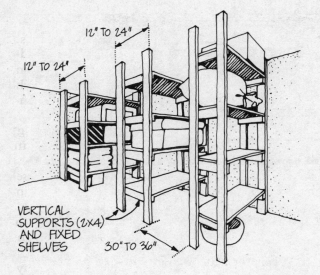

Figure 5 Maximum use of closet storage space

3. Don't waste shelf space on only a few oversized items. Create intervening shelves for smaller pieces.

It's also possible to install shelves outside the closet proper. For example, fill out a wall indentation with shelves. A five-inch indent in a little girl's bedroom wall was shelved and lined with dolls that could sit up or stand. It became both decorative and a convenient storage space. Any gap is suitable for fill-in; a two-foot gap between refrigerator and stove provides valuable storage space. New shelves can be built on *any* vertical surface; the back panel of a freestanding bookcase is just one possibility. A window can be fitted with shelves for plants.

Space near the ceiling is a relatively unexplored territory of home storage. Since most homes today have much less storage space than those built earlier, "it is important,"

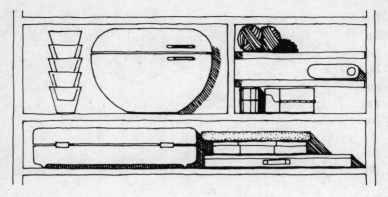

Figure 6 Storage unit with partitioned shelf space

according to decorator Milo Baughman, "to go vertically in storage pieces." (*American Home*, May 1977, p. 43). Why not build your own shelf or shelves for offseason wear, luggage, etc. starting about two feet down from the ceiling. One way to retrieve small objects from these lofty reaches, aside from the obvious stepladder or stepstool, is a "pincher," the clamp device on a long stick that is used in libraries to get books down from high shelves. If you prefer manufactured pieces, Scholfield makes "storage boxes" that can be stacked to a height of 7'10".

Hanging Space

If you don't have much to hang, individual hooks on the side of the closet or back of the door will be adequate. To create considerable new space, however, consider pegboard, the heavy perforated board on which numerous hooks can be shifted at will. Line all or part of a closet wall, or the back of the door, with pegboard. A combination of shelving and pegboard might be useful for some closets:

line the bottom half of the closet with shelves and the top half with pegboard; or shelve one wall and install pegboard on the other. A lumber yard will cut it to size, or you can buy precut pieces at a hardware store. Pegboard is cumbersome to hang because of its special screws that make a gap between the board and the wall, so make sure the installer knows his/her business.

Pegboard, like shelves, can be attached to any sturdy flat space, such as the side of a cabinet or the back of a freestanding bookcase.

Flat surfaces can be exploited even more fully if you follow the art museum practice of "skying." Rather than hanging one painting per wall section, they will hang one at eye level, one higher, and sometimes one below—thus taking advantage of the whole wall area. Consider hanging pieces that you don't ordinarily think of as hangable. A bicycle, for example, can be supported on the wall with spikes.

To make an instant supergraphic, outline the bike's shape on the wall. Hanging the bike is especially convenient in a city apartment where you don't want to leave it in the building basement. Another example of an unusual hanging idea is to nail or hook a basket to the wall to hold mending supplies or small projects next to the chair where you usually sit to watch television.

The "where do I put it?" formula: storing creatively

You may find that you are stuck with an object or category of objects that, organizationally speaking, doesn't clearly fit into an existing closet or storage area. Your tendency may be to put it randomly in the first space that will accommodate it. But once you've done that, you will probably repeat the pattern and your storage system will begin to crumble. Substitute the "get it out of sight, I'll think about it tomorrow" syndrome with a storage alternative based on the intersection between specific placement criteria and various storage techniques. There's actually a "where does it go?" formula that you can apply to any storage question: point of use × access × appropriate technique = an appropriate storage choice.

Point of use. Where do you usually use this item? A vacuum cleaner, for example, is usually used—or at least started—in the living room, so in or near the living room is a more appropriate storage place than a kitchen storage closet. Sometimes a more precise answer to the point-of-use question is appropriate. If you like to sew by the window, then sewing equipment should be stored in the window vicinity.

Or, if you take the object outside with you, where can it be reached most easily? This applies not only to keys and coats but to a bicycle or shopping cart as well. For objects that might be used anywhere—household tools, for instance—choose an arbitrary storage location, but *stick* with it.

Access. How often or urgently do you use the item on a scale of #1 to #7? Everyday use makes it a #1, once a year, #7, and the rest are somewhere in between.

Appropriate technique. With point of use and access in mind as the first two elements of the equation, consider specific storage techniques that are feasible within the chosen area and appropriately accessible: very easy to reach for a #1 object, out of the way for a #7 object, or somewhere in between.

Organizing Yourself into a New Home

If you're moving, take advantage of the best opportunity you'll ever have to organize all your closets at once, with only a fractional increase in the aggravation caused by the move itself. The suggestions that follow are also a stream-lined way to organize your closets even if you're not moving, perhaps around the time of a paint job. But don't undertake this unless your tolerance for boxes and long-term disarray is very high.

Two or three weeks before the actual moving day, examine the contents of your present closets and list basic categories. The following list is typical:

Clothing and accessories for each family member.

Toys and games (children's and adults).

Athletic equipment.

Entertainment—party goods, etc.

Coats and outerwear.

Kitchenware.

China and glass.

Linens and towels.

Miscellaneous: Luggage, extra bedding, Christmas decorations.

Souvenirs and memorabilia.

Bathroom items and toiletries.

Household supplies.

Survey the closets and cabinets in your new house,* note their location, and choose their function as described on page 122. Number each closet and make the following list of prospective contents:

Closet #1—left of entrance—coat closet.

Closet #2—right side of foyer—athletic equipment.

Closet #3—built-in cabinet in living room—entertainment (playing cards, adult games, spare ashtrays, bar glasses, liquor, ice bucket).

---

* If you're moving to another city, get a plan of the new home that includes the dimensions of all closets and cabinets. The scheme won't be as precise, but planning is still feasible.

Analyze the necessary physical adaptations (see page 126), and if possible, complete them before moving in.

Before the move, accumulate dozens of closable cartons from the movers and/or from supermarket or liquor store. (If you are dependent on store largesse, start collecting weeks before.)

Number each carton according to the closet for which it is destined—closet #1, #2, etc. Mark a separate set of cartons for the kitchen, since moving a kitchen has some special features (see page 176), and then start packing. As you move systematically from one closet in your present house to another, put the contents of each into the appropriate cartons, culling giveaways and throwaways as you work. Clothes can be packed in suitcases, or the movers will give you standing carton closets. Tag each suitcase or carton with a closet number. Movers also provide special cartons for pictures.

Pack a suitcase or two with necessities for the first few days, and group all the rest of the cartons (the #1 boxes together, the #2 boxes together, etc.) for the movers to pick up. When you arrive at your new home, move all the cartons to their respective closets. If you weren't able to install shelves and hanging space before, do it now. Unpack the cartons in the appropriate closet, and you're moved in.

Moving summary

1. Accumulate a good number of closable cartons, starting several weeks in advance of the move.
2. Break down the contents of your present closets and cabinets into broad categories.
3. Go to your new home, or work from a plan, to decide which category will be stored in each closet or cabinet. Number the closets to identify them.
4. Decide as best you can the necessary physical adapta-

tions (see page 126) and, if possible, implement them.

5. When packing, number each carton or suitcase with the appropriate closet number.
6. Complete whatever physical adaptations are necessary.
7. Unpack the cartons into the appropriate closet in your new home.

Odds and Ends

Now we come to those small but important objects that are always getting misplaced: doorkeys, glasses, the magazine you're reading, and so forth. Keys are a problem for many people. When there are a lot of them—storage room, garage, bicycle locks, lockers—set up a key rack right near the door: a wooden plaque with rows of nails, each nail labeled with the appropriate key. If you tend to misplace door keys, put a hook right near the door or keep a small bowl on a table near the entrance. Drop the keys there as soon as you come in. The bowl—or, as writer Betsy Wade put it, "the front hall bowl"—could have unlimited uses:

> With no front hall bowl, there's no place to put the letter that arrived for the people next door. There's no place to put the picture of a still-unidentified baby that fell out of a birthday card. With no front hall bowl, there's no really right place to put the skate key that is kept because when a skate key is needed, it's needed in a great hurry and there may be kids around here again anytime.*

Another variant of this idea is a "front-hall" basket or corner of the foyer table reserved for the "take-outs": the lamp to be repaired, the shoes to be resoled, the overdue library books. If you overlook, or fear you might overlook, little "to do's" on your way out—are the lights out, oven

---

*The New York Times, August 18, 1977.

off, cat not stuck in the closet—pin a checklist to the front door that you can refer to on the way out. If you have a split-level home, keep objects going upstairs or downstairs in a basket near the steps so whoever is traveling that way can take them along.

For the half-read newspaper or magazine, make a "pocket caddy" to attach to the usual reading chair: a cloth envelope out of the slipcover fabric or a compatible fabric with a long tongue fitted with snaps to attach to the chair underneath the cushion.

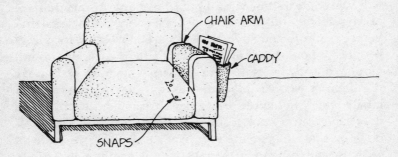

Figure 7 Chair caddy

The basic idea we are reaching for is that of convenience, which was expressed very well by Alexandra Stoddard:

> The more your organization is integrated into your every day, the more it will free your time. Have notepaper in several different locations so you can write notes spontaneously. . . . Have a shoebrush in a drawer next to your comfortable chair. What better time to buff a shoe than when you're relaxed? Have a clothesbrush on a hook in your front hall closet for the last dash out the door. . . . Everywhere you turn you should have convenience.*

*Style for Living: How to Make Where You Live You, Alexandra Stoddard (Doubleday, 1974).

9

Clothes and Accessories

Like Leslie, the harried hero/heroine of Chapter 1, a person may own a variety of clothes and yet rely on a few outfits simply because closets and drawers are in such disarray that there is no time (and little incentive) to experiment with imaginative new combinations. This chapter will explore ways to organize clothing and accessories into one workable system that will encourage more creative use.

If you share your bedroom, you probably know how irritating it is to find your partner's cufflinks in your drawer, or shirts in your closet. So the first step is to sit down and negotiate a firmly defined division of space that seems equitable to both. If you find yourself arguing over every inch, follow the provisional solution adopted by one couple: they arbitrarily divided the storage space in half, knowing that a good organizing job usually frees enough space to solve any problems. If overcrowding persisted after organizing, they agreed to renegotiate then.

Once space is allocated, move each person's belongings to the appropriate territory.

Principle #8 **When designing a personal system, first work out your "territory."**

Don't infringe thereafter on your partner's turf, and should he or she infringe on yours, define your lines without acrimony and maintain them firmly. *Don't* try to organize your partner's things.

Next, look at your closet. Over the years it may have become a receptacle for many things besides clothes: games, old toys, ten-year-old checkbooks. Weed out all these items, following the guidelines for Stage 2 (page 123). Then go through all your closets and drawers, one at a time, pulling out the articles that you haven't worn for the past year—except for the pieces that have genuine value for you, sentimental or otherwise—to give to a charity thrift shop. Don't, however, hang on to clothing that "might come in handy someday." That phrase is an instant cue to dump.

Pull out coats and outerwear for the coat closet and transfer offseason wear (summerwear in winter, winterwear in summer) to less accessible storage areas; perhaps under the bed, packed in the underbed storage units carried by department store "closet shops," which are also handy for extra bedding. One client packed offseason clothes into infrequently used suitcases. A closet shelf too high for regular use is another possibility. Other storage suggestions are outlined on page 132.

If you plan to paint your drawers and closet shelves or line them with fresh paper, this is the time to do it.

Clothes

First, decide which clothes to hang in closets and which to fold into drawers, and shift them accordingly. I recommend hanging as many articles as you have room for, including sweaters (on padded, shaped hangers), blouses, and shirts. Seeing clothes in a row before your eyes helps you to envision creative alternatives. If, on the other hand, drawer space is generous while closets are limited, drawers can be used in unusual ways. One client folded all her slacks into drawers but, rather than just stacking them, we laid them out flat with an edge of each pair showing—like cards laid out for solitaire—making them easily visible and accessible.

To organize drawers, allocate each article according to the formula, "How often do I use it?" The most frequently used items, like underwear, should be most accessible. Sweaters (unless they are hung), shirts, and sportswear are generally next; nightwear, which is changed less often, can go into the bottom drawer. Subdivide some categories—sweaters, or filmy lingerie and ordinary underwear—into their natural divisions of "frequently worn" and "less frequently worn."

If bedroom logistics permit, locate your dresser close enough to the closet so you can see both places at the same time. It's easier to create new outfits when everything is in view.

To create additional drawer space, if space or money do not permit buying a new dresser, utilize some free bookcase shelves. Curtain or screen the space if you'd like.

Also consider stackable plastic or vinyl storage cubes. For more ideas about increasing shelf space, see Chapter 8, page 132.

Arrange clothing in the closet so that articles of the same type are hanging together. Four simple categories are listed below.

For the top half of the body:	Sweaters
	Light jackets
	Blazers
	Blouses
	Shirts
For the bottom half of the body:	Slacks
	Skirts
For the whole body:	Dresses
	Men's suits
Special occasion wear:	

You'll note there is no category for "women's suits." I prefer hanging jackets with the other tops, and bottoms with the rest of the slacks or skirts. This helps liberate these articles from the "suit" restriction and allows you to consider their mix-and-match potential. If, on the other hand, you have no imagination about clothes and don't want to develop more, hang as a set the two or three outfits that you *know* go together.

Garment bags are awkward, take up valuable space, and block clothing from view. I recommend them only for extremely fragile clothing like lace or chiffon. The closet itself protects clothing from ordinary dust, and the dry cleaner's plastic bag is good protection for clothing that is particularly lint-prone.

If, after culling and organizing, the closet is still jammed, here are a few alternative ways to increase your closet space:

1. The multiple hangers that permit hanging a group of skirts, pants, or shirts do save space, but I personally find them cumbersome. If you can use them comfortably, by all means take advantage of them.
2. If there is space in the bedroom, buy a freestanding wardrobe or armoire as a second closet.
3. Buy a freestanding clothes rack such as stores use. It can be hidden with a decorative screen.
4. If your closet is deep enough, install a parallel second rack to double the hanging space. Put the clothing combinations that you wear most often in the front, and clothing worn less often in the back.
5. If your closet ceiling is high, make two layers of clothes racks: one at normal level, the other higher up. The high rack can be used either for offseason storage or, if you take advantage of the expensive long hangers, all the time. If the closet isn't high enough for two sets of full-length clothes, use the top layer just for blouses, shirts, and jackets.
6. Execute the same idea outside the closet proper. If you have an alcove from five to seven feet wide that you use for desk or work space, install a clothes rack or tension rod above your head for blouses, shirts, and jackets.
7. For a smaller alcove or indentation, buy two tension rods for two layers of half-length clothes, or one rod for full-length clothes. Cover the alcove with a curtain or screen.

Accessories

Closet designers have never discovered a really good way to handle such accessories as belts, shoes, hats, handbags, scarves, gloves, and jewelry. You're bound to be disappointed if you buy lots of boxes, containers, and "organizers" in the wistful hope that they will somehow *make* you organized. They won't, without a plan behind them.

However, boxes and various containers can be helpful if you use them thoughtfully and imaginatively. The suggestions that follow present alternatives for you to mix and match according to the kind of space you have available, and the kind and quality of accessories for which you need storage:

1. If your closet is lined with shelves, get or make boxes with a flap that falls when the cover is lifted so the contents are easy to reach. See-through shoeboxes with similar flaps are also available; they can be stored on closet shelves or stacked in a corner of the room.

2. A shoebag hung on the back of the closet door or on a side wall can also hold stockings, scarves, gloves, or rolled-up belts.

3. Buy a freestanding cabinet or cupboard with shelves for hats, handbags, and shoes.

4. There are hangers specially fitted with pockets to hold handbags or shoes. Try them if you have a lot of hanging space. Check that the plastic pockets are sturdy enough not to tear easily.

5. Get a shoe rack for the closet floor. This keeps the shoes in good order and also inhibits the tendency to throw other items on the floor.

6. For scarves, gloves, handkerchiefs, underwear, stockings, and jewelry—just about any small accessory—buy a low chest, wicker or quilted, for the bottom of the closet. If you fold your pants over hangers rather than hanging them full-length, you can accommodate quite a high chest. Leave some open space to hang full-length evening wear.

7. Line the lower portion of the closet with shelves for shoes and bags.

8. Pegboard the sides, door, and ceiling of a closet to hang shoebags, belts, ties, hats, totes, and purses.

9. Buy pronged hangers for neckties and belts.

10. Hang belts, ties, neckchains, beads, and hats on the floor-to-ceiling poles made for hanging plants, or along the branches of a decorative coat tree.
11. For belts, insert the small hooks intended to hang kitchen cups along the branches of a coat tree.

    Hooks could also work for necklaces and chains, scarves, or sweaters with a "hanging band."

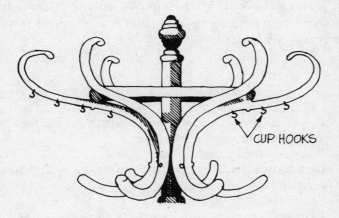

CUP HOOKS

Figure 8 Hang your accessories from a coat rack

12. There are special hangers for belts, ties, bags, neckchains, and necklaces.
13. Hang jewelry on nails on the closet walls or, if you have a nice sense of design, on the bedroom wall itself. A collection of bright purses and totes hung on the wall is also attractive.
14. Decorative hats might look nice piled on top of each other on a free tabletop or in a basket on the floor. Or consider using a milliner's hat rack.

Keep it Moving

Once organized, a clothing system is a circulating system; new things in, old clothes out. In the fall, when you put away your summer clothes, set aside those items that weren't worn that season and give them away. The chances are very good that you will wear them even less, if ever, next year. Clothes tend not to improve with age. Glance too over shoes, bags, and accessories. That is all that's necessary to stay on top of your system.

Clothes-Handling Summary

1. Divide closet and drawer space with your partner.
2. Weed nonclothing out of closets.
3. Weed out old or underused clothes.
4. Distribute offseason wear and outerwear to appropriate places.
5. Execute spruce-up projects.
6. Distribute clothes into drawers or closets.
7. Organize drawers by access.
8. Organize hanging clothes by clothing types.
9. Add new closet space if necessary.
10. Organize accessories.
11. Cull clothes twice a year at the change of seasons.

Questions & Answers

Various specific problems crop up to puzzle many people. Here are some questions that have been posed to me:

Q: *I start throwing things around when I'm in a hurry, so the system falls apart.*

A: I've alleviated my own tendency to let clothes drop

where they may (whether I'm in a hurry or not) by choosing one chair in my bedroom—a "junk chair"—on which to throw clothes or anything else that I don't feel like putting away. Putting all litter on that one chair—*not* strewing it around the room or stashing it randomly in drawers or closets—keeps things under control.

Clear off the chair at least every three days. At first, if necessary, actually write "clearing" dates in your appointment book—say, fifteen minutes twice a week—until the activity becomes a habit.

Q: *Where do I put clothes from the dry cleaners, or new clothes?*

A: Put a hook on the bedroom wall to hang dry cleaning. Put it away when you straighten out the junk chair and throw tray (see the next question). Put packages of new clothes on the junk chair.

Q: *I tend to leave small things like tie clasps and cuff links on the dresser. They soon become a depressing clutter.*

A: Keep a small tray, a "throw tray," on your dresser for cufflinks, watch, the jewelry you wore that day, and other bits and pieces. In other words, the "junk chair" idea made small. Clear out the tray every three days or so.

Q: *My closets and drawers are organized, but I still have trouble getting myself together in the morning.*

A: That probably means you're still fuzzy when you wake up, so plan to make the morning as automatic and decisionless as possible. Lay out clothes and accessories the night before. Set the table for breakfast, take out the nonperishables you plan to eat, and set up the coffeepot. Or plan a very simple breakfast, like one of the nutrient mixes.

Q: *I have piles of jewelry, too much to keep in one box.*

A: Pick out the pieces you wear and dispose of the ones you no longer care for. Divide the remainder: keep the cufflinks, earrings, bracelets that you wear most often in an accessible jewelry box or attractive tray. Hang necklaces and chains on nails or hooks on the wall or in the closet. Put jewelry worn less often in a box on the closet shelf.

Q: *My closet's sliding doors only open halfway, so half the closet is always blocked.*

A: Keep mix-and-match clothes of the same degree of "dress-up" on each side. Thus streetwear tops and bottoms would hang on one side, whereas sportswear tops and bottoms—jeans and T-shirts—would be on the other.

Q: *I like to make do with two or three basic outfits when I travel. How can I streamline packing?*

A: Attach a tag to the hanger of each packable article that lists the mix-and-match possibilities for that piece, as well as matchable accessories. This helps you quickly pull out the outfits you need, and streamlines dressing for everyday too.

10
Books
and
Records

Organizing books and records can actually be fun. It's an adventure to come across a book you've forgotten you owned, or a memorable recording. And, of course, your enjoyment is greater when your library or record collection is well-organized and easily accessible.

Books

Preliminaries

Choose a starting point arbitrarily; either one bookcase if you have several, or several shelves of one unit. If some of your books are piled in various places throughout your house or apartment, assemble them all before you begin.

Next decide whether certain categories of books appropriately belong in particular locations. Hefty art books, for instance, may fit only in one area of unusually high, solid shelving. Put the books presently in the "art area" into boxes and shelve the art books. Cookbooks are handy in or near the kitchen. There may be free book space in a kitchen cabinet or on top of the refrigerator, or plan to install one or two cookbook shelves in the kitchen. Save installation work until all the books have been organized.

To organize the balance of the books you will need a thick marking pen, a ladder for overhead shelves, grocery cartons for giveaways, and time. Reserve, if you can, two or three solid afternoons, rather than spreading the job out over several days. It is too easy to become discouraged (and possibly give up completely) after seeing the piles of books that are inevitably left on the floor when you take a break, so it's advisable to finish quickly. An hour a day schedule is possible, however, although not recommended. In that case, get at least five or six cartons in addition to the giveaways.

To start, count out thirty to forty books as the "work portion," or, if the shelves are already divided by panels, work within one panel. Begin with either the highest or lowest shelf of the bookcase on the far left. With a clear starting point you can easily keep track of the ground you've covered.

Organizing

1. Cull the work portion for books you may no longer want. Put them into a giveaway box for later pickup by a hospital, veteran's home, or charity thrift shop. They are a tax deductible charitable contribution so make sure you get a receipt.

2. Choose a category for the shelf you're working on. If there already is a preponderance of books on a particular subject on that shelf, choose that category if the access is appropriate. That is, an easily accessible shelf should be reserved for a frequently consulted category; categories consulted less often can be less accessible. If the access is wrong, or if there is no clear favorite, just choose a subject that corresponds to the amount of space available. The most typical home library categories include: *

Art
Biography
Current Affairs
Fiction
Gardening
Health
History
"How to"
Politics
Psychology
Reference books
Religion
"Self-help"
Social issues
Travel

3. Remove all the books that aren't in the subject category and arrange them in piles on the floor or on tabletops by category. Lay the piles in roughly alphabetical order so that "gardening" is somewhere near "history"; then you don't have to waste time later looking for a particular pile.

4. Go over the entire bookcase, book by book, to pick out all the books in the subject category. Put them in the

---

* Sometimes a book can be categorized in more than one place. Biographies of Jane Austen and Thomas Hardy might go with these authors' novels, or with other biographies. Just choose one alternative arbitrarily, and then stick with it.

work portion and, if necessary, block out another work portion if space for that category still isn't adequate. When you have finished one category always try to leave expansion space for several extra books.

5. In a large library, pulling *all* the books in a category might create an insurmountably huge pile. In that case, just pull enough for a work portion or so, and take note of where you stopped. When you begin work again, block out another work section, cull as in step #1, disperse the rest of the books into their piles, continue scouring the bookcase where you left off and file the subject category. Also look through the piles of miscellaneous books assembled at the beginning. Continue moving from shelf to shelf until that category is completely assembled.

   I prefer moving vertically up or down; others favor going sideways. Follow your preference, as long as you are consistent. If a category fills more than two work portions, you may want to make a block as shown in Figure 9.

6. Subdivide within a large category. The more common types of subdivision are:

   Art books—by artist, period, or country.

   Cookbooks—by author or national cuisine.

   Biographies—Alphabetize by name of subject.

   Fiction—Alphabetize by last name of author. Fiction can be divided into subcategories:
   novels
   "genre" novels—mysteries, science fiction, romance
   short stories
   plays
   poetry

7. Chose another category and decide its location. Access is the main determinant, but also consider its relation to the preceding category. For instance, "anthropology" might be more appropriate near "history" than "gardening." Continue with step #3 and subsequent

ONE CATEGORY
OF BOOKS IN THIS
AREA

Figure 9 Organizing your books

steps. However, before scouring the bookcase and miscellaneous books for the relevant category, first file the books, if any, that have already been piled on the floor in that category.

8. Continue until all the books are organized and there are no more books in boxes or on the floor. As you near the end, if a lack of space becomes evident, buy or build another bookcase. See p. 157 for space-expanding ideas.

If the job can be done within a couple of days, leave the book piles out when you break. Just clear enough of a path to move around in. If the job will take longer, put the books into cartons, marking which category is in which box. If there's room to fit more than one category per box, keep them in alphabetical order. Push the cartons into an out-of-the-way corner.

Finishing touches

Look over your shelves to check that books aren't crammed together too tightly and that there's room for expansion. Shift some work portions, or even whole categories, if the shift would make a smoother flow. This is also the time to build new shelves or create space for the cookbooks or other special book categories that don't belong in the regular bookcase.

It's helpful in a large library to identify the bookshelves with labels made with handheld, punch-out devices.

The streamlined plan

There is a streamlined way to organize books that I don't recommend to most people because it calls for intimidatingly large piles of books on the floor for what could be days on end. But if you are unfazed by a temporary bombed-out look, by all means consider this alternative plan.

Sketch a rough, freehand chart of all your bookshelves. Chart in hand, test each shelf for accessibility. A shelf at arm level is #1; space reached by stooping or stretching a little is #2 or #3; stretch up on tiptoe or bend all the way down for #4 or #5. Mark the chart accordingly in the style of Figure 10.

Then, starting at the lower left corner of the bookshelf, pull out all the books in the entire system, arranging them on the floor by category in roughly alphabetical order. Continue until the shelves are entirely clear. Add the miscellaneous books gathered from elsewhere in the house. Rank the categories according to your interest in them; a category of lively interest is #1, and so forth. Then file all the

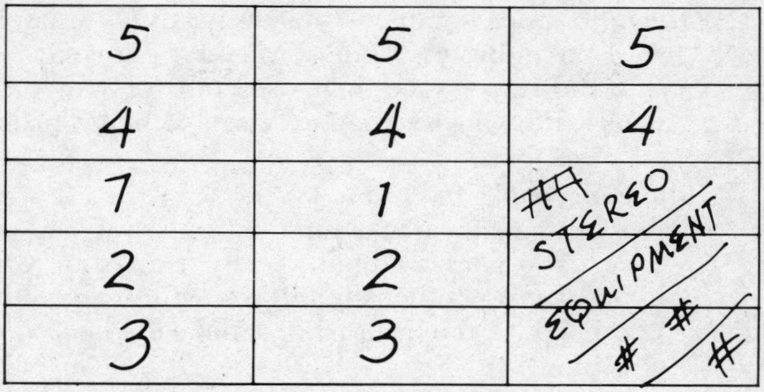

5	5	5
4	4	4
7	1	~~###~~ STEREO
2	2	EQUIPMENT
3	3	# # #

Figure 10 Bookshelves—Accessibility Chart

#1 books on #1 shelves, and so on until the library is completely reshelved and organized.

Subdivide the categories if you like according to the guidelines on page 154.

Extending book space

If there are still more books than shelf space, buy or build new shelves or look into these expansion techniques:

Get a freestanding bookcase. Either line it up against the wall or make it a room divider. If you already have a bookcase/divider, glue or bolt the new bookcase back-to-back with the first one.

Bolt a bookcase on top of an existing bookcase.

Combine handsome, vinyl stackable cubes into a wall unit or a room divider. Cubes are probably most appropriate for mixed use: books, plants, wine, etc.

Some books may be consulted so infrequently that they could be transferred to a closet shelf, or even to free space in a kitchen cabinet.

The high space in outsize shelves is largely wasted. Install an in-between shelf. Measure the space carefully, to make sure there is room for two rows of books, allowing for the shelf itself, which is probably ¾" thick.

File paperbacks in double layers. Reserve a few of the most important books for the front row, and otherwise just organize alphabetically from front to back, by subject and then by author within the subject. Loosely pack the front row to make the back row accessible.

As a general rule, don't stack books on their sides. It seems a space saver, but it effectively removes any book but the top two from circulation.

Book Organizing Summary

1. Assemble all the books you plan to organize.
2. Certain categories may belong in special locations—cookbooks in the kitchen, art books in an area of high, solid shelving. Move the books accordingly.
3. Choose a work portion (thirty to forty books, or a natural bookcase division) at the top or bottom shelf on the left.
4. Cull giveaway books from the work portion.
5. Choose a category for the work portion.
6. Remove all books from that portion except for the subject category, and arrange them by category on the floor.
7. Scour the bookcase for all subject books (unless there are great numbers—see note on page 154), and fill the designated space.
8. Continue the same category in the next shelf if more space is needed, culling out and filling in, until the category is completed.
9. Subdivide, if you like, within a large category.

10. Choose a new category for the next shelf, and begin again with step #4.
11. Check for finishing touches (p. 156) and, if you are still cramped, explore expanding storage space (p. 157).

Records and Tapes

Records and tapes are physically too different to intermix comfortably, so organize them separately. Weed out the records or tapes that you have lost interest in and give them away.

Divide what remains into categories. In many cases, this list of basic categories is adequate:

Popular	*Classical*	*Other*
Ballads	Chamber music	Folk
Country and	Opera	Jazz
Western	Orchestral music	Religious
Dance music	Soloists	music
Mood music	(instrumental)	Spoken word
Rock	Soloists (vocal)	
Show music		

Complications can arise if your emphasis is on other areas. Arranging by composer, for example—all Mozart, all Beethoven, etc.—may present a problem because many records feature works by various composers. In such case, file the record according to the composer that's most important to you. If you'd like to categorize more than one composer, make a cross-reference card; "Schubert, Fantasy in F Minor—see Beethoven, Archduke." Organize any way you wish—by composer, performer, period, instrument, whatever—so long as you are consistent in your system.

Either arrange your record or tape collection according to the one-shelf-at-a-time method recommended for books, or, if it is no larger than 200 pieces or so, try the streamlined system discussed on page 156. Maintain the organization by physically distinguishing between the various major divisions. For example, store classical records in white vinyl cubes and pop records in yellow. Or, if you store records on bookshelves, label the shelves or insert dividers between the different categories.

One special point about tapes: Commercial tapes are rarely labeled on the side so it's difficult to identify them if they are stored upright. Label them yourself if necessary.

11
Kitchen

The kitchen, more than any other room in your home, should be arranged and organized in the way that's most convenient for the user. Cramped space, poorly arranged utensils, and the need for constant trips between counter and range can dampen the enthusiasm of any cook. A well-planned scheme—the one that's best for *you*—will, on the other hand, make all kitchen work more pleasant, and so much easier that maintenance will become routine.

The process begins with a budget. An expert cook may find it worthwhile to spend several thousand dollars to gut the present kitchen and design a new one from scratch. Most people, however, have neither the interest nor skills— to say nothing of the money—to take full advantage of a custom kitchen. Think, rather, of modifying your standard kitchen (which invariably has not, in my experience, been designed with comfort and efficiency in mind), to conform to your needs. You can do a lot for several hundred dollars, and ingenious modifications can be made for $100 or less. Suggestions in this chapter run the financial gamut; choose the ideas that fit your needs and budget.

Defining Problems

Initially, define the problems you experience in your kitchen. Almost all kitchen difficulties fall into one of three categories: work area; storage; serving and clearing. Specific instances of each are:

Work area:

1. Inadequate work space. A client who baked had no room in her work area to set down a mixing bowl she had finished with, so she had to take it across the room to get it out of the way.
2. A poorly located work counter—one too far away from the storage cabinets and oven—creating constant and unnecessary movement.
3. A counter so awkwardly positioned that rolling dough becomes difficult.

Storage:

1. A shelf high enough to accommodate large appliances is otherwise largely wasted space.
2. Dishes stored so high that they become virtually unreachable.
3. Serving dishes and utensils piled so haphazardly that pieces become hard to find and reach when they are needed.

Serving and clearing:

1. Too many trips between the dining area and kitchen indicates a problem in the serving and clearing process.

If you have trouble getting down to particulars, it helps to pinpoint a *process* that causes trouble—for instance, baking pies, preparing casseroles, or clearing the table. Then walk through the motions of the process, notebook in hand, and write down the specific "sticking" points as they come up.

However you arrive at your list of problems, rank them according to how troublesome they are. After you've read the instructions in the appropriate sections for solving your particular difficulties, work your way down your list starting with the #1 problem. This chapter also covers a streamlined way to organize your kitchen when moving into a new home.

Work Area

In any kitchen, large or small, you should have a central work area that is generous, extremely compact, safe, comfortable, and easy to care for. According to Mimi Sheraton, food editor of *The New York Times*, ". . . the actual work area that includes range, sink and refrigerator should be small, so that those three major pieces of equipment are each no more than a step or pivot apart." A long walk is not only exhausting but a "downright hazard if one is draining a heavy potful of boiling water that must be carried from stove to sink." (*The New York Times*, April 20, 1977, page C4.)

If your present kitchen fails to meet this ideal, consult with your service representative to see whether the refrigerator and/or range can be moved closer together. If not, you can to some extent compensate for poorly placed appliances by substituting miniaturized versions: for example, a toaster/oven/broiler, electric frying pan, or water immersion heater kept near the sink can take the place of the less convenient range when you are preparing lunches, light meals, and snacks. You must have counter space for them, however, or be prepared to install a convenient appliance shelf.

If the main range is your only alternative, get a small wheeled cart so that you can push pots and crockery from one place to the other. If the refrigerator is off the track, an expensive but handy solution is to install a small refrigerator under the sink for milk, fruit, and a few frequently used items.

The main working counter should be large enough so that you can lay out ingredients, cut, mix, season, and prepare foods for cooking, and should be within the compact sink-range-refrigerator triangle. Counter space outside the triangle is largely wasted. To increase the efficiency of well-placed (within the triangle) counter space, keep counters as free of kitchen appliances and supplies as possible. Hang the dish drainer on the wall, and put canisters on shelves. Other storage tips are discussed later in this chapter.

Then, if necessary, improvise new counter spaces. Get a board, or have one cut, that is wide enough to span the sink but not so deep that it interferes with use of the faucets. A board roughly half the size of the sink is about right. Another solution would be to fasten a hinged board to the wall which can be lowered when needed. A wheeled cart with butcherboard top or a stationary table can also provide more counter space. They can also do double duty for dishes and utensils.

Counters should be high enough to allow you to work without bending. If they are too low, get a three-inch thick cutting board to build up counter height during extensive cutting and dicing jobs. If you are customizing, consider making the counter low enough so that you can sit while you work. In that case, your chair should be on wheels, otherwise the constant getting up and down will cause more fatigue than steady standing.

Where to put dirty dishes or utensils when counter space adjacent to the work area is insufficient is a chronic problem that causes a great deal of unnecessary movement. Rinse the dishes out if you can, or fill them with water to soak. This step is helpful even if your diswasher, if you have one, purports to clean dried-out food. Put the filled bowls and pots on the stove or in the oven if those areas are free, or install a wall shelf specifically for dirty utensils. You can also use a rolling cart, or failing that, set them on newspaper in a corner on the floor.

Put dirty spoons and small implements on a little tray especially curved to hold spoons, teabags, and other small messy items. Collect parings, bruised leaves, and scrapings on a paper towel, so as not to clutter the counter, and throw them out all at once. One client hooked a plastic flowerpot onto the wall for that purpose, and emptied it into the compost heap when it filled.

A relatively maintenance-free kitchen is, in general, one where furniture and fittings have smooth, simple shapes, and floors and cabinets demand only a swipe from damp mop or sponge.

Storage

Arrange to devote about an hour a day for a week or so to kitchen storage, first clearing out the deadwood, then planning and executing solutions. Go through each drawer and shelf noting unnecessary duplications (three can openers?), and apply the basic "to keep or not to keep" test to any doubtful objects:

1. Have I used this item within the past year?
2. If not, do I want to keep it anyway because it's beautiful or because it has value (sentimental or monetary)?
3. If not, might it come in handy someday?

Don't get caught by saying "maybe" to question 3. Toss the eggbeater, or whatever. You'll buy another one if you must. As always, store the excess in grocery cartons for giveaway.

Next, consider whether more kitchen storage space could be opened up by transferring some items nearer to their point of use. For example, if you generally serve dinner at the table, shift the dishes and silver as close to the eating area as possible to make table-setting less of a chore. Remove some glasses to the living room and operate your bar out of that room instead of the kitchen. This procedure not only releases kitchen space, but saves a lot of trips from kitchen to living or dining area.

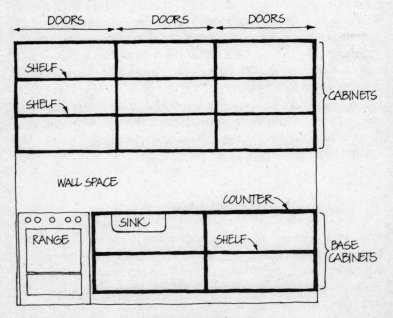

Figure 11 Kitchen—Accessibility Chart I

Charting

If the reorganization job is full-scale, chart your kitchen space to define its accessibility. Choose one of the kitchen walls to start with, open all cabinets and drawers on that wall above and below the counter, and sketch a very rough, freehand, unmeasured diagram of all the shelves, drawers, and surfaces. Indicate the wall itself and cabinet doors. Do this for the entire kitchen. Figure 11 is a sample.

Next, extend your hand to all the shelves, drawers, and surfaces on each wall. Space directly in front of your hand is #1; #2 space is accessible with a small stretch; #3 space is fairly accessible; and space that requires use of a step-ladder is #10. The front section of a shelf may be #1 or #2, while the less accessible rear is #3 or #4. Judge these spaces

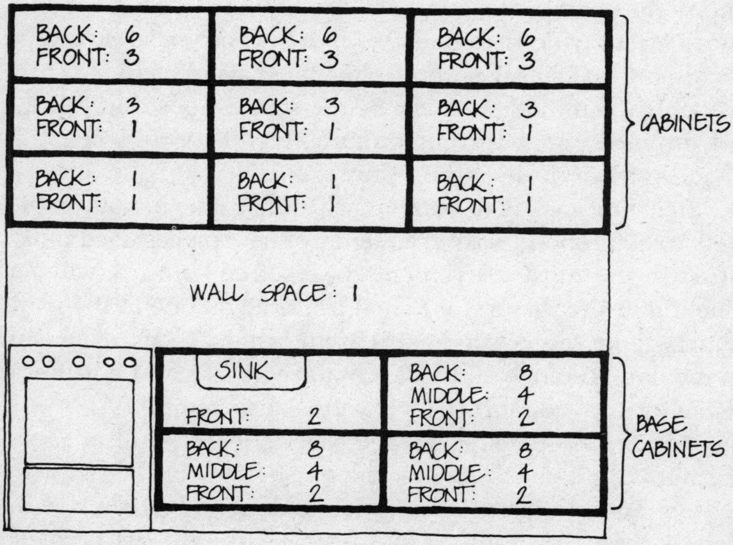

Figure 12   Kitchen—Accessibility Chart II

according to your own comfort, not against some hypothetical ideal. A lithe person, for example, could rank a bending-down space as #2, while the same space might rank #4 or #5 for someone less agile.

Write the rank number of every shelf and surface on the diagram. The sample might now look like Figure 12.

Getting the most from what you've got

Organize the spaces that already exist before considering construction possibilities. In any organizing job it's generally wise to utilize as fully as possible all existing facilities before making any major changes or additions.

Start with the cabinets. According to a government pamphlet, *Designing for Safety* (#2300–00266), the *top* of a kitchen cabinet should rise six feet from the floor, not too far above eye level for people of average height, and shelves should be on ball bearings so they can be pulled out. Would that it were true. In actuality, kitchen cabinets are usually rigid and invariably so high that most people can get full use only from the first shelf. So the suggestions that follow are intended to wrest maximum flexibility and responsiveness from these clumsy units.

The first task is to rearrange all the items in your cabinets to correspond with frequency of use; pieces used most often in the most convenient spaces, and so on down the line. Examine the first #1 shelf as noted on one of the wall charts, and reserve it for all items that are used nearly every day. Remove all pieces that are not #1 and put them aside for the moment. This is your "unsorted pile."

Next, look through all the other shelves, pull out any #1 items, and put them into the #1 shelf space that was released. Follow this procedure for each of the #1 shelves in your kitchen until all #1 shelves contain only #1 objects, and no #1 objects are inappropriately placed. If you have room to spread out do so, but don't worry if—the more likely situation—utensils are fairly crammed at this point. Cramming will be dealt with when we get to working out more efficient ways to use space. At present, proper placement is top priority.

Turn next to the #2 shelves and follow the same procedure:

1. Leave #2 items—things used several times a week—in place on the shelf.
2. Remove items that are not #2 and put with the unsorted pile.
3. Scout the remaining shelves for #2 items and add them to the appropriate shelves.
4. Pick any #2 items out of the unsorted pile and put them on the #2 shelves.

Shift the remaining items the same way according to this scale: #3 pieces are used pretty regularly, #4 fairly often, #5 occasionally, #6 seldom, and so on. Put the final items—the #10's, like the big once-a-year Thanksgiving roasting pan—in a #10 space atop the cabinets or on a high closet shelf.

As you place utensils, also ask yourself "Where do I stand when I use this object?" or "Where do I *first* use this object?" and pinpoint that location as closely as you can. Store the most frequently used serving bowls, platters, and serving spoons within the range-refrigerator-sink triangle, so food can be transferred smoothly from cooking pot to serving utensil. If you cook and serve from the same vessel, so much the better.

Materials that are used only together should be clustered together; for example, baking items like cake flour, rolling pin, sifter. Since mixing bowls are generally used for other purposes as well, store them with other bowls.

One tip: all china of the same pattern need not be stored together. Divide place settings. If, for example, you are a family of four and have service for twelve, put half of the dishes on a higher shelf, or even in a cabinet in another room.

Once utensils are properly located, consider more efficient utilization of the shelves themselves. Shelves are often too deep (a twelve-inch depth is about right) and almost always too high. One way to solve this problem is to insert portable shelf racks to make two functional shelves out of one that is semifunctional. Some shelf racks divide the space more or less evenly; others create a low space for small jars and a higher one for glasses or cans. Evaluate your shelf height and your needs before deciding what to buy. There are also revolving shelves that can hold cans, spices, or small dishes.

Dish organizers use shelf space quite efficiently. There are two styles: one type stacks small and larger plates horizontally on different levels and provides cup hooks. The other type, which I find easier to handle, stores plates in an upright position.

Other freestanding (that is, not requiring installation) "organizers" can serve a variety of purposes; for example, you can "file" those floppy pouches of beans, soups, or dried foods in a narrow box organizer. There is a useful organizer for pot and casserole covers, and holders for aluminum foil, plastic wrap, and other paper supplies. Organizers are also very helpful in putting wasted space to use, whether it's the typical cavern under the sink or an empty corner. You can get organizers for cleaning supplies and paper goods, and storage bins for potatoes, onions, canned goods, or even large pots or appliances. Some storage bins fit on runners to make drawers. Arrange them all, of course, according to frequency of use.

Also consider stackable plastic or vinyl storage cubes for dishes, glasses, rolls of plastic wrap and aluminum foil. Baskets can hold canned goods or dry food. Cluster baskets in a corner or, in a large kitchen, line them up to make a room divider. The empty sections in a freestanding wine rack could be used for rolled-up towels, napkins, or table-cloths.

Whichever organizer(s) you choose, a few unused inches often remain at the top of the shelf. Screw in some hooks for cups or small gadgets, making sure, however, that you can still remove items easily. Cramming only leads to disorganization, so if you have the space to spread out, stack no more than three pieces on top of each other.

Counters can also provide storage space if they are wide enough. Line them with canisters of sugar or flour, cookie jars, or jugs to hold "bouquets" of small utensils like serving spoons and spatulas. Small appliances like blenders will also fit on a wide counter.

Use drawers for silverware, towels, staple vegetables like potatoes or onions, or fitted as a breadbox. Keep small utensils in drawers only if there is enough space so they don't jumble. Otherwise hang them with magnetic hooks, pegboard, or keep them in jugs.

Organize your refrigerator like any other cabinet, keeping frequently used items closest to hand, and group-ing together similar foods such as different types of cheeses. Choose a particular corner for leftovers so that you will no-tice them before they spoil. If bottles don't fill your high main compartment, divide the space with shelf-makers. A shelf might enlarge the freezer capacity too. If you buy a new refrigerator, purchase one with pull-out or revolving shelves that will enable you to reach the back easily. The most convenient freezers that I have seen are at the bottom of the unit, or in compartments lining the side, rather than the traditional box across the top. With this layout the vegetable bin is placed at the top, making it much more accessible.

Making new storage space

If cabinets and drawers are still overcrowded after sorting and placing, hanging and shelving are two space-extending techniques.

Hangable pieces include pots and pans of every description, cups, pitchers, small utensils like wire whisks, spatulas and slotted spoons, scissors, pot holders, paper towel holders, and even plates and platters. Almost any utensil can be made hangable. I have drilled holes in many things, including a rubber dishdrainer tray, a Dutch oven, and a small lucite cutting board. For one very large cutting board that was too thick to fit a hook, I put a strong keychain in the hole to hang it from.

If you plan to hang a number of items, pegboard, which opens a great amount of space, is the most efficient solution. It can be hung, cut to size or in precut pieces, on any flat surface, including walls, cabinet doors both inside and outside, the sides of cabinets and counters, and the undersides of cabinets. In other words, every inch of surface is a potential hanging space. It helps to paint an outline around each object on pegboard so you'll know where it goes—and whether you've hung it up or not!

Other hanging ideas include:

Magnetized hooks for small utensils. Make the refrigerator door a household message center by leaving little notes under magnets. Also dry plastic bags by slipping a small magnet inside each bag and hanging it on a metal surface.

Pin or hook a *permanent* pad and pen in an accessible

location. Jot down any food or household item when you notice stocks running low. Take the slip with you to the supermarket, along with slips from other supply areas (see page 222).

Hang large pots, pans, and baskets from a cast-iron or steel ceiling fixture, or directly from ceiling hooks. One client attached a basketball hoop above the work counter, lined with "S" hooks (hooks shaped like an "S"), and hung all her spatulas and light utensils so they were easily accessible.

Put hooks on the underside of kitchen cabinets for cups, mugs, and small gadgets. A rack specifically for wineglasses and other stemware that attaches under a cabinet is available. The glasses are stored upside down, and can be slid out. There is a similar rack for cups. There are other types of upside-down arrangements for glasses too, such as those you see in bars. They would have to be custom-made.

Hanging "organizers" of various kinds is useful. Here are a few suggestions: spice racks; knife holders; paper bag or garbage bag holders; paper towel holders; plastic wrap and wax paper holders; a wire rack hooked inside the undersink cabinet door for dishwashing liquid and cleansing powders. Make your own organizer for extra bottles with six-pack beer or soda cartons. A long, narrow wicker basket, of the type to hold rolls, is also good for spices.

One tip on spices that also applies to canned goods: alphabetize them! It sounds a little compulsive, but it makes small bottles or cans very easy to find.

Creating extra shelf space is the other main extension technique. For instance, install a shelf in the gap between counter and cabinet, or between refrigerator and stove. Insert a shelf between two existing shelves if the height is unusually generous. Don't waste high shelf space that might be used for only one or two tall objects. Add another partial shelf to store small items in that space as well. Shelve a tall, narrow broom closet and hang the broom and dustpan on the wall. One client shelved a five inch deep indentation in the wall, creating #1 space for canned goods.

Bulk storage

If you have the space, buy food in quantity at a considerably lower price. To store perishables, I recommend a freezer shaped like a refrigerator, as opposed to the older style "chest" freezer. To clarify, this is not a refrigerator freezing compartment, but a full-sized appliance that freezes food for up to a year. Make sure that the freezer has pull-out shelves to keep foods in the rear from getting iced in.

Label each shelf: "meats," "vegetables," "fruits," "prepared foods." Wrap each package in freezer paper and label the outside, stating contents of the package and date of freezing. Put freshly packaged foods in the back of the freezer and keep moving older foods up toward the front.

A storeroom or pantry for dry and canned foods is a great advantage; you can sometimes buy wholesale if the quantity is large enough. At the very least, take advantage of supermarket specials, and also buy the largest size available, which is usually more economical. Divide the "large economy size" box into smaller containers that will fit on your kitchen shelves. The storeroom itself should be organized like any other shelf space.

Serving and Clearing

The simplest way to swiftly transfer dishes from kitchen to table is a mobile serving cart. Load it with clean dishes to set the table, dirty dishes during and after the meal, and push it to the sink. A mobile cart, by eliminating multiple trips between kitchen and patio or barbecue, is especially convenient for eating outdoors.

Some people solve eating-serving-and-clearing problems by building a connecting counter between kitchen and dining area. This is helpful only when kitchen and dining room adjoin one another so that food and dirty dishes are accessible to both locations, and can be passed back and forth easily.

A good counter can also offer fringe benefits: snack bar, storage area, and sometimes an additional working counter. These are the specifications to create these extra amenities:

If you would like to make it a working counter, construct two levels—a level low enough to sit at comfortably for light meals, and a higher level to stand and work at. Alternatively, make the eating level a retractable shelf that you can pull out for meals. If you don't need another working surface, make the counter the lower height.

Figure the counter's width by measuring the thigh-joint-to-knee length of the household's tallest person, and add the diameter of your dinner plates plus a few extra inches.

Leave enough open space on the kitchen side for someone to sit comfortably with legs underneath as in a coffeeshop (that is, the thigh-joint-to-knee length).

Make the dining side into an open-shelf cabinet for storing dinnerware, possibly liquor, and some serving pieces. (Reminder: Keep frequently used pieces on the kitchen side.) If you don't need a snacking counter create storage space on both the kitchen and dining sides. Or incorporate both ideas by making a shelf that pulls out when needed for snacks and light meals.

Organizing into a New Home

Moving presents a great opportunity to organize your entire kitchen at once. In fact, this streamlined technique can be used even if you're not moving, but don't try it unless you know you won't get bogged down in the middle. Collect lots of grocery cartons and mark one box "K#1" ("K" meaning "kitchen"), another box "K#2," and so on through "K#5." Mark a sixth box "K#6 and up." Also have giveaway and throwaway boxes on hand. Go through your kitchen cabinets and drawers piece by piece and winnow and evaluate each object as discussed on page 166. Put aside enough basic pieces to use until you're set up in your new kitchen—plates, can opener, coffee, etc.—and distribute everything else: #1 pieces in the #1 box, #2 pieces in the #2 box, and so on. As you fill each box, label its contents. *Do not* combine differently ranked items in one box, even if the #2 box is full while #5 has extra space. This only creates extra work.

When you get to your new kitchen, sketch and rank the spaces as discussed on page 167, and start unpacking the "#6 and up" items first. Try to stack no more than three objects on top of each other, other than sets. If space becomes too tight as you reach the #2 or #3 items, plan how to expand the space according to the techniques discussed in this chapter, and execute the job.

12
Rooms in General

Your living room is a disaster area. The neighbors came over to see the ballgame, but only two people could watch the set at one time. The stereo was on the coffee table for lack of an alternative, so the only place to put drinks was on the floor. Two drinks were knocked over. You tried to put the Monopoly set away after a rousing game but the closet where you generally store board games is full. At least the family has been trained to stash games in one corner. Unfortunately, the game corner is the place where you had been practicing Yoga.

If anything in this story sounds familiar, you are suffering from "room overload"; the natural, though not inevitable, consequence of a room—whether called living room, den, family room, or recreation room—that functions in multiple ways. The flexibility that makes such a room the center of family operations also makes it particularly susceptible to the kind of disarray that is impractical and difficult to live with.

If room overload is your problem, utilize the suggestions that follow to design a workable, comfortable area. If, on the other hand, your room only has a few problem spots, read the chapter through once and then turn to page 187 for pointers on solving spot problems.

Clearing the Room

In order to come to grips with miscellaneous clutter, block out and concentrate on an area approximately five feet square. Take a critical look at every object or category of objects (except furniture) in that space to decide whether it belongs in the room at all. If the objects go elsewhere, distribute them appropriately: papers and old magazines to the desk to be sorted and integrated into the paperhandling system (see Chapter 5, page 67); toys and games to the children's rooms; rainhats to the closet. Don't try organizing the closet or shelf you're distributing *to*, just fit the items in as best you can. Put objects that do belong in the room near related objects—stack books in or near the bookcase, for example. Survey and distribute the contents of the entire living room methodically in this fashion.

Some items will frustrate you because they don't seem to have a natural "home." For example:

Ashtrays (extras).
Card table.
Coasters.
Folding chairs.
Games.

Liquor and accessories.
Magazines.
Matches.
Plant care or pet care items.
Serving trays.
Snack or candy dishes.

A wall system—a combination of cabinetry and shelving that lines all or part of a wall—could handle most of these items. If you do get a wall system, buy a unit that accommodates the specific articles you intend to store. If, for example, liquor storage is no problem, a built-in bar is wasted space. Wall units are, however, generally quite expensive and sometimes overwhelm a small room. If space is a prime consideration and you prefer more modest arrangements, see Chapter 8, page 132 for a discussion of tight-space storage techniques. Also see Chapter 13, page 199 for tips on choosing storage units.

What People Do in the Room

An important step in organizing any room is choosing that room's appropriate functions. Often, "room overload" is a result of allowing too many activities to go on in one single room. Narrowing the list frees space and allows you to enjoy your room in greater comfort. The list that follows includes most activities that might go on in a living room:

Children playing.
Conversation.
Drinking (alcohol).
Eating (meals and/or snacks).
Entertaining.
Exercising.
Games (cards, Scrabble).

Hobbies.
Housecleaning.
Music (piano, guitar, stereo).
Reading.
Telephoning.
Sewing, knitting.
Sleeping (nighttime—convertible couch or daybed).
Sleeping (napping).
Stereo or radio listening.
Storage.
Television viewing.

_____

_____

Check off the activities that are performed in your room. Use the extra lines to write in pursuits not listed.

Relocating activities

Some of these activities might be more profitably moved to another part of the house if any of the following criteria apply:

An activity interferes with other functions. For example, children who are playing may disturb adults.

An activity would be more convenient elsewhere. For example, some china and glassware may have been stored in the living room because that's where you put it when you first moved in. Ideally, it should be nearer the kitchen or dining room.

The activity annoys you. For example, it might irritate you to see your husband or wife napping on the couch.

Head a sheet of paper "Project List #1," list the activity to be relocated, and the specific steps necessary to do so. For example:

Children playing. The television set may be drawing them to the living room. If so, you might get the kids their own TV, or put the TV in their playroom. If books, games, and toys are stored in the living room, you might want to move them to the children's room.

China and glassware. Transferring these items to the kitchen or dining room is the main step, but list preliminary steps: for example, consolidating the kitchen cabinets to make additional space, or getting a new stand-up cabinet for the kitchen. (Make very simple kitchen changes at this time; just enough to accommodate the items as best you can. You'll organize china and glassware when you do the kitchen. See page 168.)

Napping on the couch. If a request to nap in the bedroom isn't effective, consider exchanging the present capacious couch which invites slumber for a smaller loveseat. Alternatively, the modification may be in the bedroom rather than the living room. Perhaps the bed's satin coverlet discourages casual napping. If so, list on Project List #1 whatever can be done quickly—"buy wool throw to protect bedspread"— and postpone a large-scale bedroom planning job. This postponement is an important element of all organizing.

Principle #9 **Organize one thing at a time. Save organizing further trouble spots until later.**

In addition to moving some activities out, there are others that might be brought in. One client, for example, exercised every morning in a cramped bedroom corner only rendered operational by pushing a chair out of the way, although the living room contained a larger, more convenient open space. After our consultation, the living room became the exercise site. To make the change feasible, my client bought a tall, cylindrical basket to hold the rolled-up tatami mat, and installed some hooks inside the nearby closet where she could hang her leotard and jump rope.

Consider additional activities that might benefit you and add them to the basic activities list. List on Project List #1 the specific steps needed to make the shift.

Finally, action. Execute all the projects on PL#1 and throw the list away.

Defining Problems

Return to the Activities List on page 179 and check off those functions that aren't working well in the room. In order to arrive at a solution, define and analyze the problem activities. Let's take two functions of our hypothetical living room as an example: conversation/small-scale entertainment, and children playing. You'll need a fresh sheet of paper, Project List #2, as your problem list.

Conversation/small-scale entertaining

Visualize your family with a guest or two sitting in the room. Are there enough seats for everybody? Must chairs be brought from other parts of the room? If seating isn't adequate write "more seating" on Project List #2. Are the seats comfortable? What about lighting? Too bright or too dim?

Is the furniture arrangement conducive to conversation? Do people have to lean forward to hear one another? Can they see each other without obstruction? Must people balance snacks on their knees because there's no convenient place to put them? Consider the same set of questions for a larger group of people—four to twelve—if you have, or would like to have, frequent guests. Note each problem on PL#2. Don't work on solutions yet; just note that the problems exist.

Children playing

If you enjoy having the entire family together, thereby encouraging the children to stay around, there are probably going to be problems. The most likely are:

Noise.
Breakage of valuables.
Spills and stains on rugs and furntiture.
Clutter.
Interference with adult conversation and activities.

List these and any other specific problems on Project List #2.

Analyzing activities: checklist

The two activities analyzed above illustrate a procedure that can be applied to virtually any awkward situation, whether it's a single spot problem or one of the troublesome activities on your activities list. Here is a summary of the activity-analysis process:

1. Visualize the activity in your mind.
2. Analyze the scene for physical comfort. For instance, are the chairs at the table high enough to permit eating in comfort? Can people easily interact with one another? Is there enough light, and is it placed properly for the activity?

3. Are people engaged comfortably with *things?* Can all TV watchers see the screen?
4. Is the furniture *appropriate* to the activity? Should a spindly-legged Louix XV ottoman hold the feet of a 6-foot tall, 180-pound man?
5. What accessories would make the activity more comfortable? A reading chair, for instance, might be enhanced by a magazine rack, snack table, ottoman, and/or adjustable lamp. Also see page 123 for a reminder about keeping the things you use close to hand.
6. Is the activity convenient to a related area? A dining table, for example, should be near the kitchen.

List the problem's components on Project List #2.

Making the Room Work

Most of the problems defined on PL#2 will yield any number of possible solutions ranging from clever and inexpensive gimmicks to costly new pieces of furniture. Decide in advance approximately how much money you can spend to alter the room so you can choose realistically between alternatives. Begin then with a fresh sheet of paper headed Project List #3 and list the exact steps—purchases, moves, modifications—needed to solve the problem. As you define solutions, cross the activity off PL#2. To illustrate how this process works, let's consider the two room functions discussed earlier:

Conversation/small-scale entertaining

Let's assume for the sake of illustration that your present conversation area is inadequate in the extreme. These are the problems listed on PL#2:

More seating needed.

Uncomfortable upright chair.

The glass over the painting causes glare.

The couch and the chairs are too far apart;
    people chatting have to raise their voices.

People sitting on the couch have no place
    to set plates or drinks.

Step by step, list your proposed solutions on Project
List #3.

More seating needed: Folding chairs is one idea, but
you're probably looking for a permanent arrangement, not
a solution for the occasional party or large gathering.* You
can enlarge the conversational area by replacing chairs
with a couch or loveseat, either bought new or taken from
another part of the house. Two couches facing one another,
with chairs in between, create an attractive area. Use either traditional couches and chairs or the contemporary
"modular" furniture that is especially designed to create
shiftable conversation groups. Alternatively, big floor pillows, if they are compatible with your decor, make attractive and handy seating. Nesting chairs are a good back-up
idea: light, stackable chairs, usually rattan or straw, that
can be kept unobtrusively in a corner. Make two conversation groupings in a fairly large room by placing two sofas
back to back and adding other chairs around each sofa.
This can comfortably accommodate quite a few people.

Upright chair uncomfortable: Perhaps add a cushion.
Alternatively, get a more comfortable seat for the conversation grouping and use the upright chair primarily for
decoration.

Glaring light on glass: Try spraying the glass with a
nonglare solution. If that doesn't work, consider moving
the painting or the lamp.

* See the bibliography for books that cover the subject of parties and
    large-scale entertainment.

Couch and chairs too far apart: Before you rearrange them—the obvious solution—decide why you originally put them so far apart. Did you want, for example, to make a passageway from one side of the room to the other? If so, perhaps the entire conversation area could be moved to another spot in the room. Or the coffee table might be too big, creating the unnecessary distance. A decision is in order then: could the table be used elsewhere? Could the furniture be arranged on two contiguous sides? Mark your steps on PL #3 and also note supplemental moves needed to accommodate the changes—moving end tables, lamps, etc.

Snacks and drinks: End tables, the obvious solution, can run into money. Try building them: wooden boxes, measured to fit the height and depth of the couch, with laminated butcherboard tops. Allow for a generous surface area. Paint the front and sides or cover with patterned contact paper. Another inexpensive idea is to build or buy small round masonite tables and cover them with tablecloths. (See page 203 for more on end tables.) If space for permanent end tables is a problem, fit some "occasional" tables with caster wheels so they can be moved easily to serve as snack tables when the occasion arises.

Rearranging a conversational area can offer unexpected benefits. One client mentioned that his teen-aged children rearely spent the evening with the family. After we rearranged the room, it became so pleasant that the children began joining in. A conversation grouping will encourage conversation.

Children playing

Project List #2 listed these disadvantages of children playing in the living room:

Noise.
Breakage of valuables.

Spills and stains on rugs and furniture.
Clutter.
Interference with adult conversation
 and activities.

Noise is a discipline problem, not an organizing problem, but if even normal noise seems jarring, check acoustics. An uncarpeted floor will sometimes cause noise to reverberate. Also check ceiling acoustics. Mark any project on Project List #3.

To prevent breakage, remove fragile items to high shelves. Sturdy furniture is imperative; an antique-filled room is not a good candidate for playroom.

You can't prevent spills or stains, but you can dilute their effect by protecting furniture with vinyls, glazed chintzes, or other relatively childproof fabrics. Sew sturdy snaps to the couch or chair in an unobtrusive site—the back of a pillow or the back of a chair—and snap on attractive but inexpensive full-sized throws. They can be taken off when you have company.

Interference with adult activities is, to some extent, what you're opting for, but don't let children take over. Stock a corner with toys, games, drawing papers and pens, and maybe a television set. Line an accessible shelf or table with cork or vinyl to set glasses of milk down on. The children's corner should provide enough shelf and cabinet space to store their things. (See also "Children's Rooms," page 230.)

Checklist: making changes

The examples we've considered illustrate the thought processes involved in creating a functional, pleasant room. The following checklist summarizes these steps briefly.

STEP 1. Read quickly over Project List #2—your list of room activities broken down into specific problem areas.

STEP 2. Head a fresh sheet of paper "Project List #3."

STEP 3. Consider the first problem on PL#2. If a solution is obvious, mark it on PL#3. If not, ask yourself these questions:

    a. Can a substitute object fulfill the same function more effectively? For example, stretching a seating area by substituting a couch for two chairs.

    b. Could an object or piece of furniture be made more comfortable, or otherwise modified?

    c. Is a simple shifting of furniture or objects the answer?

    d. Will new furniture or objects solve the problem?

    e. If storage is your problem, will a major project like buying a wall unit or building more shelves be best, or might more modest alternatives (see pages 130–136) answer the need?

    f. Can the problem be alleviated by creating *new* storage spaces?

    g. Would protective slipcovers or flooring help?

    h. Would caster wheels make furniture more mobile, thereby creating more space?

STEP 4. Write down on Project List #3 the exact steps needed to solve all the problem points in the first two activities. Include all relevant measurements. Cross the activities off Project List #2.

STEP 5. Actually implement all changes for the first two activities.

STEP 6. When Step 5 seems well under control, define solutions for the next two activities and implement them. Continue the "define/implement" pattern until the room is completed.

The Model Room

Although this procedure is optional, if problems are so numerous that a complete revamping seems in order, including major furniture purchases, it might help clarify your alternatives to plan everything in advance by designing a model room on paper.

The procedure calls for several sheets of graph paper, some brightly colored construction paper (get two colors), a fine-point black marker and a fine-point colored marker, a ruler, a yardstick and/or tape measure, a scissors, and a compass to draw circles.

After first measuring the dimensions of your room, including alcoves and ells, outline the room with the black marker on graph paper at a scale of one inch to one foot. Also indicate to scale, with the *colored* marker, doors, windows, and structural features like radiators, built-in bookshelves, and fireplace. Note how far the radiators jut out into the room.

The illustration on the next page is a sample plan.

Next, measure width and length of each piece of furniture that rests on the floor. For circular furniture, measure the diameter.* Outline the furniture on the construction paper, using one color and the same one-foot-to-one-inch scale. Cut the pieces out and label each piece.

Check Project List #3 for pieces of furniture that you propose to buy. Estimate their measurements and cut them out of the other shade of construction paper. Then consult Project List #3, one activity at a time, to solve each problem by moving around the cutouts, both the existing pieces and the provisional ones, on the graph paper. Some activities can be doubled up—for example, a conversation area

---

* To measure diameter, run a tape measure from one point on the circle to another across the center.

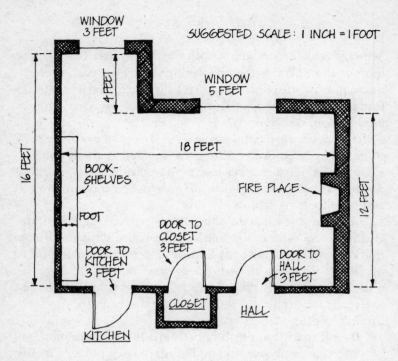

Figure 13   Design a model room on paper

can be adapted to snacking—but doubling is not always desirable. A large room may call for a spread-out design to fill otherwise overlarge spaces. Make sure that pathways are wide enough, and that people aren't bumping into furniture on the way from one room to another.

When the scheme seems satisfactory, attach each cutout to the graph paper with a sliver of scotch tape and put it away for a few days. During the interval, jot down any new ideas on Project List #3. When you take the plan out again, incorporate new ideas or revise it as you see fit. Finally, confirm the plan by evaluating it as pure design. An effective plan will always look "shapely" and should convey a sense of balance.

Even if the scheme isn't yet perfect stay with what you have. This is an important principle:

Principle #10 **If invention has run dry, execute the less than perfect solution. A more satisfactory answer will generally come to you in time.**

Now physically execute the design in your room to conform to the plan.

The Well-Organized Room—
A Master Checklist

1. Clear the room of clutter (page 178).
2. List all the activities that go on in the room (page 179).
3. Decide which activities belong in the room and which don't, and take steps to shift them using Project List #1 (page 180). Correct the Activities List accordingly.
4. Analyze each activity into specific problems areas and list the problems on Project List #2. (See discussion on pages 182–184 and the "Activities Analysis Checklist" on page 183.)
5. Decide how much money you are willing to spend.
6. Work out solutions and list them on Project List #3. See the discussion on pages 184–187, and then follow the "Making Changes Checklist" on page 187.
7. Optional. If alternatives are confusing or if you plan a large-scale revamping, design a model room on paper (page 189).
8. Walk through the room to check that you can move smoothly from one area to another. Also consider scale

and size. Is furniture too big for the room? Is there too much furniture or too many accessories? If the flow of space is a severe problem, see the discussion on flexible rooms (Chapter 13, page 198).

13

Rooms
in Particular

Some rooms—bathrooms, bedrooms, multiple-use rooms (studio apartments or lofts), and workrooms—are used in specialized ways. This chapter analyzes layout and storage problems specific to those rooms.

Bathroom

Many people draw a blank when they consider organizing the bathroom. What to do with all the bottles and tubes? And you can't rearrange the furniture. It is possible, however, to get around the almost invariably awkward bathroom setup by judicious use of one "bathroom aid" or another.

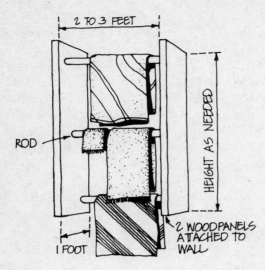
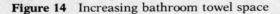

Figure 14 Increasing bathroom towel space

For bathing and showering, reduce the sense of "invasion by shampoo bottle" by consolidating all the paraphernalia on a bathtub tray, shower caddy, or shelf inside the tub. There are also shower curtains with pockets for shampoo and soap. Add no-slip stripping in the tub for safety.

If you have a small bathroom, a big family, and a shortage of towel racks, put towel hooks on the wall or create several towel racks in a limited space by attaching two one-foot panels three feet apart to the bathroom wall, and connect the panels by staggered rods.

Bathroom storage—cosmetics and supplies

Begin by working systematically from medicine chest to toilet ledge to windowsills to bathtub to shelves, ruth-

lessly discarding all the items you don't use anymore—
even expensive cosmetics. Divide whatever is left over into
three categories: utilitarian, grooming/cosmetic, and storage.

Utilitarian products like Band-Aids, aspirin, and medicines can be stored in the medicine chest, along with deo-
dorants and other grooming articles not attractive enough
for display. Put extra supplies of any item in the storage
group. If you have many medicines, alphabetize them. Arrange the medicine chest so that items used most
frequently are most accessible. Also keep first aid instructions immediately handy. Once a month, check the cabinet
and throw out any product you've stopped using.

Grooming/cosmetic items include, for both men and
women, skin care products, hair products, colognes and
perfumes, bath powders, and makeup. Cosmetic items can
be attractively displayed on a two-or-three-shelf wall rack
on the most accessible wall, or in an accessory shelf on the
window. If these ideas are not feasible, put them on top of
the toilet ledge or on a windowsill. To expedite cleaning
the ledge or sill, stand the jars up in straw baskets with
sides just high enough to keep the jars from toppling over.
Keep small articles like tubes of lipstick, rouge, and eye
shadows in small boxes or baskets. Stand elongated pieces
like mascara wands in plastic cups. (This is also a good idea
for thermometers, small tubes of liniment, etc.) About once
a month, when you check the medicine chest, glance over
the cosmetics and throw out whatever isn't being used.

Storage items include backup stocks of toothpaste,
soap, cosmetics, and toilet paper, plus bathroom cleansing
products like soapsuds, powders, and toilet bowl cleaners.
Utilize whatever fairly accessible space exists nearby; a
linen closet in the hall, a clothes closet shelf, or even an
unused dresser drawer can provide sufficient storage. If you
are ambitious, build a wall cabinet or an undersink cabi-

net. An *ad hoc* undersink storage area can be made by lining the sink with a skirt and putting in a couple of Rubbermaid "instant shelves." The same skirted space can be used as a clothes hamper; put down a rubber pad so clothes don't get thrown directly on the floor.

Towels and linens are discussed in Chapter 14.

Bedroom

To make the bedroom an especially comfortable haven, plan to make the bed the center of operations. First, consider the bed itself. A loft bed, double or single, practically doubles usable space in a small room by leaving space below for office, dressing room, closet, or sitting area. Platform beds, fitted with big drawers for extra bedding or off-season clothes, are coming into their own as a new kind of storage facility. If you have an ordinary bed and the room is too narrow for a bedside night table, place the bed on the diagonal and fit the open corner with shelves. It's also easier to make a bed when it's not pushed against the wall.

Next, list all activities conducted from the bed. Possibilities include:

Cosmetic operations: makeup, nails, etc.

Eating: snacking, breakfast in bed.

Games or cards.

Hobbies: sketching, stamp collecting, etc.

Home office: letters, bills.

Intimacies.

Phoning.

Reading.

Sewing, knitting.

Stereo or radio.

Television.

Analyze your chosen activities according to the procedure outlined in Chapter 12, page 183, and list the various accessories you'll need. Many of them—a nail care kit, a can of peanuts, playing cards—will fit into one or two commodious end tables, the simplest storage solution, plus a basket under the bed for projects. Baskets, either hung from a wall hook or set on the floor, are helpful for odds and ends. A wall hook is also a place to hang a mending or knitting satchel.

A handy way to accommodate spillover is an under-the-bed "dolly." Build a plywood box about three-feet square with sides two inches high—just high enough so objects won't fall out. Knot a four-foot length of clothesline or light rope through a hole drilled in one side, and tie the other end of the line to the bed framework near your hand as you sit in bed. Set the dolly on casters and pull it out whenever you want it. A dolly is especially useful for items such as phone books, knitting bag, and writing supplies.

Headboards can provide storage too, from a simple set of built-in night tables to elaborate units fitted with lights, bookshelves, stereo compartment, and even a false top that lifts to reveal a storage compartment for extra blankets and pillows. The furthest extreme of headboard development is the "environment," equipped with stereo, lights, mirrors, television, and even a bar.

Failing an elaborate headboard, stand current books and magazines on the night table, toss them into a straw bedside basket, or make or buy a bed caddy: a cloth envelope secured to the bed by slipping a long flap between mattress and springs. Prop yourself up to read with a bolster, either a full "armchair" type or an abbreviated armchair. Some bolsters have pockets for pencils, paperbacks, etc. A late-night reader, whose spouse goes to sleep earlier, can switch from a regular reading lamp to a small, high-intensity lamp that clips to the book and only illuminates the page.

Why not set up a bedside system for simple paperwork, such as bills and personal letters? (A more complex home office has its own rules of organization as discussed in Chapter 4.) One client put two handsome pots by her bedside: the brass pot was "to do" and the copper pot, "to file." A night table basket held notepaper, envelopes, checkbook, stamps, pens, and her organizing calendar. We hung a clipboard on a hook by the bed. File cabinets and backup supplies were in another room.

Carry out the same idea by nailing two baskets, "to do" and "to file," to the wall, using a portable caddy for the paraphernalia.

Stereos and tape decks are a problem if you want to be able to use them from the bed. Setting them on a night table blocks too much space, so build a shelf low enough that you can turn the set off just as you doze off, but placed so you don't bump into it when you sit up.

Studio Apartments and Other Small Spaces

Studio apartments present a special organizational challenge: how to extract full value from every inch of space in order to comfortably lead a full life in a small room that retains an open "feel." (There are also useful tips in this section for a large loft or any undifferentiated space.)

Partitions

Your first decision is whether or not to physically separate the three main household functions—eating, sleeping, and "living"—by partitioning the space. There are three styles of partitions: full and permanent, mobile, and partial. A permanent partition is usually expensive and is difficult to remove once in place. Consider this alternative only if your room is very large, otherwise you'll lose any sense of space. One permanent option is a sliding door or a roll-up, floor-to-ceiling screen, which combines certain features of permanence (it must be installed), and mobility (it can be easily whisked out of sight).

Less expensively, a bank of stacked plastic or vinyl storage cubes or a high bookcase will create separate rooms as adequately as a floor-to-ceiling partition if sound is not a factor. Paint the back of a freestanding bookcase, or sheath it with fabric or pegboard. To increase shelf space, shelve the back panel of the bookcase, or glue or bolt two bookcases back to back. There is another bookcase idea that can give shape to a featureless room while creating a coat closet and storage area. Build a floor-to-ceiling unit that's shelved on one side and flat on the other. Fit a tension rod between the flat side and the wall to make coat-hanging space. Build high shelves above the rod for out-of-the-way storage. See Figure 15 for the design.*

Consider where to locate a permanent partition, and what kind to get, in terms of the following criteria:

1. "Room" size. Don't be too hasty to set up a minuscule bedroom. If a tiny room will make you claustrophobic you might do better not to divide at all, or to divide the rooms more equitably.
2. Unfettered movement through the apartment. Make sure that the proposed partitions don't block your normal movements from area to area.
3. Light. Unless the partition can be opened, like a drape or shade, be careful to place it so as not to cut off sources of light.
4. Storage capabilities. A more elaborate version of the bookcase/storage cube idea is a new modular wall sys-

* From an idea in *Better Homes and Gardens*, July, 1977.

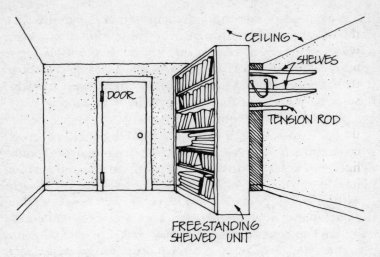

Figure 15 Use of a divider to define and increase space

tem called "Expanda-walls," produced by Charlton, that rolls freely on concealed casters, and can form right angles or outside curves, or serve as room dividers or corner units.

Much the same criteria apply to open or partial dividers. They won't make separate rooms, but they can both unify and define areas in an attractive way. A row or cluster of large plants or baskets works well, and a serving counter between kitchen and dining area is useful for both definition and storage. Define two living room areas—a conversation/TV area and an eating section—with open shelfwork that also creates space for books, plants, and decorative pieces. The two-sided structure is handsome and useful. I've seen a freestanding fireplace accessible to both living room and dining room, each side stocked with its own wood and implements.

Light, mobile partitions that you can shift at will are the simplest solution. One attractive variety are the opaque white screens found at Japanese variety stores (for example, Azuma in New York). There are also burlap screens that you can cover with fabric or marbleized paper. Put screens on casters for greater mobility.

You might even have some ready-made room divisions that you hadn't thought to take advantage of. Make an alcove into a small, self-contained "reading room." Convert a hall closet into a mini-office. A wide, underused closet can be converted to a seating alcove or desk area. These are examples of what is called "adaptive re-use." If a space is obstructed by a door, either rehang the door to open in the opposite direction or remove it altogether.

Divide vertical space too. Make a loft in an old high-ceilinged house or apartment—not merely a loft bed, but an actual small room on the second level. A loft seven feet or nine feet might do for a small office; install a dining area in an 8-foot-by-ten-foot loft, with pulleys to hoist dishes and food. Create an actual small bedroom. And of course the space below is released for whatever purpose you have in mind.

Using furniture to save space

Once you've decided how or whether to partition the room, consider how to exploit space to the fullest without clutter. (See also the discussion of compact storage in Chapter 8.) Thoughtful furniture selection and placement is the key. Run through your activities as defined in Chapter 12, page 179, and list the basic furniture and accessories needed for each activity. Are there pieces of furniture on your list that can be entirely eliminated through canny storage techniques? People tend to assume, for instance, that they must have a dresser. But some of the storage techniques in Chapter 9 might create enough new shelf space to eliminate the need for a dresser. In other words, think of the function rather than the piece of furniture. Consider too, whether you can adapt small pieces to serve the same function as furniture that may be too large for a small space. The functions of a big desk, for example, might be met by a narrower parsons table for a writing surface, backed up by a file cabinet in the closet and a portable caddy to hold supplies.

Next consider what functions can be combined in one piece of furniture. Modular furniture is the ultimate in multifunctional units: all-purpose, interchangeable modules that can be clustered into conversational groupings, opened into "pits," formed into couches or sleeping spaces, used as tables, or just about anything the imagination can devise.* However, the traditional framework of tables, chairs, and couches can be extremely flexible and spacesaving. One single table, for instance, can triple as a dining table for six or eight, desk, sewing table, or even a bed (see bed/table below). You can either get a full-sized table big enough for all purposes, or a fold-up piece. There is one floor cabinet on the market** that opens into a dining table for six, and when closed, can store chairs, tablecloths, glassware, and almost anything else you can think of. Nesting tables are, of course, a tried and true space-saving table idea.

The basic combination piece is the traditional convertible couch—still usually the most convenient sleeping alternative for a fairly traditional room. Another good idea is

---

* Drexel manufactures a fairly high-priced version of these systems. More casual and less expensive lines are made by Dunning, Ltd., and Bunting, Inc. Addresses for these and the other furniture manufacturers mentioned are listed on page 241.
** Manufactured by Raymor Moreddi.

the daybed, a single bed covered with a throw and some pillows. It functions as a couch during the day and a bed at night. Some versions are fitted with a "trundle bed" that can be slid out to make a double bed. The "Nap Sack" is a chair that stretches into a bed.*

Another bed combination idea is the bed/table. Measure a standard cot mattress and cut wood to that size. Set it on legs twenty-nine inches high—the standard table height. When company comes, roll out the cot mattress or a sleeping bag and you have an extra bed. Otherwise the shelf serves as combination table/buffet/desk. Alternatively, attach the bed/table *sturdily* to the wall on hinges and fold it up when not in use.

The most famous disappearing bed is the built-in Murphy bed,** but I think there is somewhat less efficiency there than meets the eye. The bed's wall area is virtually unusable for anything else, and, when let down, the bed takes up considerable floor space.

Before you commit yourself to any piece that expands, opens, or otherwise changes position, particularly an expensive one, think through the space it occupies when open. Will it displace other furniture? If so, it might be worth putting either the expandable piece or the displaced pieces on casters, or choose a less bothersome alternative.

Selecting furniture or decorative pieces that can double as storage units is another way to get the most from limited space. Cluster large, covered baskets, for example, which can hold offseason clothes, linens, dry or canned foods, in a corner with plants, or use them as end tables, telephone table, or ottomans when topped with cushions. For end tables and/or coffee tables consider steamer trunks or, if your decor is contemporary, white or brightly colored

* Manufactured by Domani division, Burris Industries.
** Manufactured by Murphy Beds and Kitchen Co., Raynes, Inc.

lateral-drawer filing cabinets with a laminated butcher-board cut to size and glued on top. It sounds unusual, but it is handsome and practical. Put heavy materials in the bottom drawer to keep the cabinets steady.

A wicker chest is another coffee table or end table idea. Covered with cushions, a wicker chest becomes a window seat. Make a more elaborate window seat by constructing a window ledge banquette that lifts up like a piano bench to provide immense storage space. Another construction idea is to make platforms fitted with huge drawers to serve as a base for seating or sleeping. Make a three-part table with a hinged top as the centerpiece that raises to reveal a bin underneath suitable as storage for yarns, fabric, or extra bedding.

If you have a table with a lower shelf, cover the table with a cloth and use that shelf to store offseason clothes or an extra blanket.

Another comparatively neglected aspect of comfortable small-space living is thoughtful furniture placement. A small room is only tolerable when there is easy move-

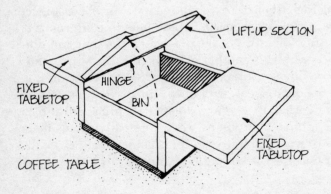

Figure 16 Multiple use of furniture

ment within it, and I personally favor at least one open space five feet square. The heart of placement is to create blocks of furniture that either touch or are linked in some way, thus opening floor space. For example, back a couch with a dining table/desk as pictured in Figure 17.

Select chairs that don't jut out; possibly mobile stools that can be pushed under the table when not in use. The big table also doubles as a coffee table and end tables, thus obviating the need for additional furniture in that area. The two easy chairs opposite the couch are linked by a single side table.

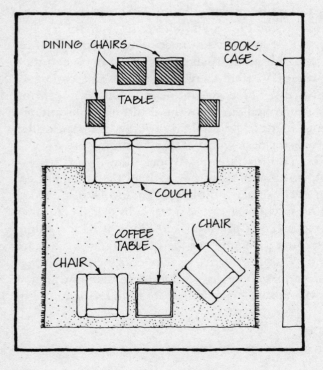

Figure 17 A furniture arrangement for Small-Scale Living

To define two conversation areas, place two couches back to back. Another back-to-back idea is a headboard substitute for a daybed. To read in bed, prop yourself against a drop-leaf table, a high-backed dining bench, the back of a sturdy stacking cube storage arrangement, or the back of a bookcase or room divider.

Consolidate furniture in vertical space as well: hang a swinging chair from the ceiling, and keep a wicker storage chest beneath it. Or sling a hammock diagonally between two corners and put a low bookcase underneath. The space behind the bookcase could be a storage corner. Tuck mobile stools and tables under other tables.

The final element in small space living is mobility: furniture that can be produced as needed and then deftly hidden away or made unobtrusive again. The most common answer is wheels. Virtually any piece of furniture can be set on caster wheels. Some specific ideas include: a serving table or trolley rolled out from the wall for drinks and entertainment fixings; individual rolling snack tables; wheeled stools for desk, vanity table, or dining table.

Another mobility idea is "knock down" furniture— pieces that are assembled as needed and then dismantled. For example, construct a table on demand from plywood boards set on sawhorses; or top a tall cylindrical container with a round piece of plywood and drape it with a tablecloth. This same principle can be used to make a square table round. There is also the swivel principle: a long-necked wall lamp can be directed to more than one area; a swivel television set is viewable from both living and dining areas.

Studio apartment checklist

1. Decide whether to partition off the eating, sleeping, and "living" areas.

2. If so, evaluate the type of partition to get and its placement in terms of:
   a. "Room" size.
   b. Movement within the apartment.
   c. Light.
   d. Storage capabilities.
   e. Consider alternative partitions: closets, alcoves, vertical space.
3. Within the basic "area" divisions, or within the apartment as a whole, consider techniques for extracting full use of space:
   a. Elimination of unnecessary pieces of furniture.
   b. Furniture with more than one function.
   c. Fold-up or tuckaway furniture.
   d. Furniture as storage.
   e. Furniture placement.
   f. Mobility.

Workrooms: Artwork, Carpentry, Sewing

Any workroom requires three main elements: a surface to work on, a place for materials and implements, and storage arrangements. The principles for arranging your particular setup are the same in any case, so you can generalize from the examples that follow to your own situation.

1. Processes. List the exact processes that are entailed in your work. Sewing processes include laying out and pinning up patterns, sewing by machine, sewing by hand. A handyman cuts wood (sawing? by machine?), hammers, drills, and paints.
2. Work Surface. Most work requires one main work surface, although a person who sews needs two: one for pinning up patterns and one for sewing. To define the work surface(s) you require, check your process list and ask the following questions about each item:

    a. Do I stand or sit? If you stand, make the table or drawing board high enough to stand at upright; if you sit, the table should accommodate a comfortable, upright sitting position. If either or both, would a table that can be raised or lowered suit the purpose? Or two different tables? In that case, you might put the lower table on casters to slide under the higher table.

    b. To define the appropriate size of the table (if it's not standard like a drawing table) consider the size of the materials you're working with: a pattern, a "mechanical" for book designers, long pieces of wood. Have the table or counter cut somewhat bigger than you anticipate. If several processes are involved, as in handywork, the table should be long enough to accommodate each process.

3. "Placement" surface. A placement surface should be the right size to hold the tools or materials that you'll need as you work, and located so that you hardly need change position to lay something down on it. Perhaps an "ell" as pictured in Figure 18.

4. Chair. The chair should be comfortable, support your back, and preferably swivel so you can switch position

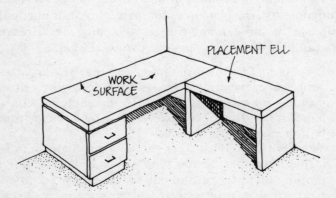

Figure 18 Increasing work space

easily. It shouldn't be too broad, or its arms, if any, too high, to scoot right in to the work surface.

5. Lighting. Natural light, if you can arrange it, is best for your eyes. Artificial light should fully illuminate the work area without glaring. Choose a lamp—whether placed on the ceiling, table, or wall—with a mobile neck that can be adjusted to whatever job you're doing.

6. Storing supplies. Stand or sit in working position and go through the motions of each process listed in step 1. Place the most frequently used supplies or tools for each process wherever your hand rests most naturally. To pin up patterns, for example, hang the scissors on a wall hook right by the table, or perhaps dangling from a nail on the table itself. Hang a box of pins in the same way.

Figure 19   Wall storage for hobby supplies

For sewing supplies and fabrics there are plastic bins that fit together on runners to make drawers. Keep them under the sewing table. If you knit, hang your skeins from rods affixed on a wooden plaque that hangs on the wall, and make compartments for rolls of yarn. The most common solution for handywork tools is pegboard; outline each tool so you know where to put it back. The pegboard should back the work table or form an ell, whichever is more accessible. It would also be helpful to have shelves or cabinets for jars of nails, screws, and other small pieces, as well as for tools that won't hang. Shelve the wall, perhaps above the placement ell, or underneath the work surface. Another solution is a rolling cart kept under the work counter when not in use. The cart should be high enough to eliminate bending down for the frequently used pieces. When you've organized your tools and supplies, fill a few small jars with the most frequently used nails and screws. Keep them on the work counter or nail the tops of the jars to the underside of a convenient shelf.

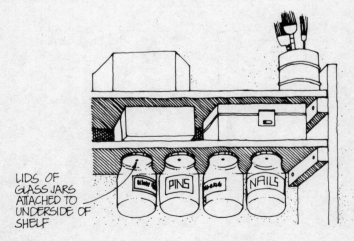

LIDS OF GLASS JARS ATTACHED TO UNDERSIDE OF SHELF

PINS   NAILS

Figure 20 Increased use of limited space

Replenish the small jars from a larger jar when supplies run low.

7. Putting projects away. At the end of a work session, it's
depressing to leave the materials you have been working with lying around, particularly if you're working
on more than one project. For sewing storage, buy a set
of low, deep shelves. Art supply stores are likely to have
something appropriate. Attach a peel-off label to each
shelf for the life of the project and remove it when the
project is finished. To keep track of several projects, list
each item you're working on, a deadline if any, and
what stage it is in. Pin the list to the wall or bulletin
board and bring it up to date each time you work. The
same idea applies to artwork or handywork projects.

The plastic cabinets mentioned above are ideal for
storing artwork. That is actually what they are intended for. Construction projects are bigger and thus
somewhat more complicated. I suggest shelves on the
wall. Use full-length shelves for large projects, and divide some shelves vertically in half, or even in thirds
for smaller projects. Label each section with the name
of the project using peel-off labels. Separate bins for
each project would also be satisfactory; in that case,
stock each project bin with a few smaller boxes to
maintain control of small pieces such as joints and
hinges.

14
The Efficient Home

A modest degree of order in the home—a necessity for a reasonably comfortable life—consists of a moderately clean house; a simple system for shopping, food preparation, errands and laundry; and a plan for shared family participation in these tasks for both parents and childless couples.

Cleaning the House

Cleaning can provide a modest sort of pleasure. It's good exercise, can be mindlessly involving and, unlike most efforts in this complicated world, provides a clear and unambiguous sense of accomplishment.

The most crucial step is to set up a cleaning schedule that you follow faithfully. Start by setting an arbitrary hour a day, either early in the morning or later, even after work, depending on your energy levels. The hour should be divided as follows:

Layer 1

These are the jobs that must be done every day: making beds, washing dishes, reducing clutter, dusting lightly, taking out the garbage, and cleaning ashtrays. List these jobs on a sheet of paper and time yourself while doing them. Subtract any time spent on the phone or with other interruptions.

Layer 1 tasks should take no longer than half an hour in a one-bedroom home. Add ten minutes for each additional bedroom, and ten minutes if there are two floors in your house. If you have difficulty meeting this time limit, analyze how the work might be streamlined:

1. Are you trying to do too many of the jobs yourself? Should the children, for instance, be making their own beds and picking up after themselves?
2. Are the materials and supplies you need instantly available, either in mobile caddies or strategically placed storage points?
3. How are you handling interruptions (see page 48)? Are you distracting yourself?

Here are some tips for some of the specific jobs involved in layer 1:

Picking up. No matter how organized your home is, certain activities do create a trail of debris. Store all leftovers in one unused drawer, closet, shelf, or basket, so that all the miscellany is in one place. Anyone in the family who sees something out of place should add it to the pile for later sorting. Supply a small box for little objects like keys or jewelry.

When clutter is more than minor—guests have spent the evening for example—tidy up "around the clock" so to speak. Choose a starting point anywhere on the perimeter of the room and think of it as twelve o'clock. Straighten it up completely, move to one o'clock, and continue around the room. Then straighten up the center. It's a good idea to trundle a mobile cart along with you to collect items that belong in other rooms, saving trips back and forth.

In a two-story house, keep a basket at the top of the stairs and one at the bottom where you can deposit objects belonging on the other floor. It's always a good idea, in fact, to train yourself to pick up, as you move from one room to another, the items that belong where you're going.

Layer 2

These are twice-a-week (more or less) projects, including vacuuming, watering plants, wiping down the bathroom, sweeping floors. List the Layer 2's and then arbitrarily work on them in sequence for one-half hour only. Begin the next day where you left off and again work for half an hour. When you finish the sequence once, start it over again. Follow the procedure for a week and keep track of how often you do each task. If it's approximately twice during the week, that's fine; more than twice is more often than the task requires. Gradually shorten the length of time per day you devote to Layer 2 tasks until you meet the twice-a-week schedule.

Some tips follow for making these jobs easier:

Vacuuming. Using two vacuum cleaners may be helpful; a light cleaner for your weekly routine and a heavy-duty cleaner for a thorough once-monthly cleanup. If you are allergic to dust, lint, or pet hairs, check into the powerful, built-in vacuums that suck the dirt through tubes in the wall to an outside container that is emptied about every six weeks. A big plus from an efficiency point of view is that you get rid of the cumbersome canister trundling behind. Check your local vacuum cleaner supply firm.

Always vacuum before you dust since the dust stirred by the cleaner might land on furniture you've just dusted.

Watering plants. You can save time here by only keeping plants that thrive with a twice-a-week watering. However, if your preferences range over a spectrum of plants, attach colored dots on the pots to signify each plant's watering needs: a yellow sticker for daily watering, blue for weekly, and so on. Then, depending on their light requirements, try to group plants with the same watering requirements together. Keep a *large* watering can and mister in the kitchen and, if there are plants upstairs or in other areas of the house, keep another set in a bathroom.

You might try using travel bulbs. These are water-filled bulbs put into the soil to keep the plant moist for up to three weeks. They reduce the need for watering considerably, and I've been told that plants requiring continuous moisture thrive on this regime.

Bathroom. Hang a sponge on a hook right above the sink. Encourage family members to give the sink a swipe after each use.

If you take frequent tub baths use bath salts that dissolve "bathtub ring." If you shower, cut down on residue by maintaining freeflowing drains.

Investigate toilet bowl solutions that keep toilets permanently clean.

Layer 3 and Layer 4

Layer 3 jobs are the "deep cleaning," once-a-week operations: scrubbing floors, waxing and polishing furniture, cleaning walls and woodwork, grocery shopping, errands, and laundry chores. You can tackle these in several ways. You can set aside several hours a week to do all the jobs at once—Saturday morning is a popular choice; you can add one layer 3 job to your regular cleaning schedule each day; or when it seems necessary, add a particular task to your "To do" list for the following day.

Layer 4 consists of special projects: washing windows, cleaning the stove, defrosting the refrigerator, polishing silver, and so forth. Either choose a fixed two hours a week to devote to special projects, or add them to the "To do" list as they come up.

After experimenting and streamlining your own individual routine, write up a final cleaning schedule similar to the one below.

Layer 1:	making beds washing dishes picking up dusting taking out garbage	a half hour per day every day
Layer 2:	vacuuming watering plants wiping down bathroom sweeping floors	a half hour per day in sequence
Layer 3:	mopping floors polishing furniture walls and woodwork groceries errands laundry	Saturday morning
Layer 4:	special projects	on To Do list when necessary

Meal Planning

Once a week should be often enough for the planning of family meals. You might refer to your local newspaper to see what foods are specially priced for that week. As you decide on the menus, list whatever ingredients are not on hand.

Drawing up the weekly menu/shopping list takes about an hour, but there is an easy way to reduce it to about ten or fifteen minutes by making up menu cards. Compile, from your favorite recipes, twenty to thirty easy-to-prepare main dishes. Write out or scotchtape each recipe to a five-by-eight-inch index card and note any ingredients you might have to buy at a special shop. Then, copy about thirty recipes for side dishes and desserts, and file all the cards in a file box. Each week select as many main dish cards as necessary, mix and match them with different side dishes and desserts, and there are your menus. List the ingredients you don't have on hand, add staples like salad fixings, bread, and beverages, and you're ready for the supermarket.

Working people will find it helpful to patronize a market where all or part of a grocery order can be phoned in for later pickup or delivery. The shopping that you do yourself can be greatly streamlined by designing a categorized grocery list. Write or type the following categories on a sheet of 8½-by-11-inch paper, leaving some space between each category:

Dairy products
Canned fruits, vegetables, juices
Fresh produce
Fresh meats and fish
Canned goods

Frozen goods
Breads and baked goods
Spices and condiments
Household goods
Any other category: pet foods, etc.

Arrange the categories on your master list according to your normal supermarket route. If your first stop is the meat counter, meat is the first category on your form.

Have a trial run through the supermarket with the list, make any changes that are necessary, and then have it xeroxed or made up in quantity in tablet or pad form with a hole in the top so you can hang it on a hook in the kitchen, readily available. Fill in the form whenever you notice low stock on a particular item, and complete the fill-in when you plan your weekly menus.

To further streamline shopping, unload your goods onto the checkout counter as they are arranged at home: all refrigerator items together, all canned vegetables, etc. The checker won't place them in perfect order, but there will be a rough approximation. It's surprising how much this will simplify unpacking and putting away at home.

Precook stews and casseroles, or prepackage the ingredients—each meal packaged separately—and freeze.

Freeze small leftover portions in individual containers so that you can pop them into the oven for a quick lunch or an afterschool snack for the children. Label each package with freezer labels and keep packages that have been frozen for longer periods moving toward the front. Get pots large enough for quantity cooking, and be sure to have enough freezer containers. Freezing meals in freezer-to-oven-to-table ware saves a lot of dishwashing. See page 174 for some recommendations on freezers.

Shopping

If you consider clothes shopping a chore, why not plan to shop in a single department store that carries the greatest range of merchandise that appeals to you. This concentration of shopping saves time, and if you have difficulty making decisions, automatically limits your alternatives. It is especially helpful to establish a relationship with one salesperson who gets to know your style and taste. Such a relationship has many advantages and can save you both time and money. The salesperson will sometimes hold a particular item aside until it goes on sale, phone you when new shipments come in, advise you on special values, prevent you from wasting a trip to the store when there's nothing there to your taste and even, in certain stores, select clothes to be sent to your home "on approval."

When you go to the store, take a list of planned purchases—main items and accessories. One woman I know shops by imagining occasions that will occur in the forthcoming season: a business meeting, a cocktail party, and so forth. She then examines her existing wardrobe for any article of clothing that might form a "core" piece. When she stops she takes that article and a list of the things she intends to buy to supplement the "core" piece. This system saves time and lessens the dilemma of having a closetful of clothes but nothing to wear.

Try to confine "serious" shopping to one or two expeditions at spring and fall, with occasional "fill-ins" during the rest of the year. To make the spring and fall forays even more productive, list all the birthday and anniversary presents that will be coming up during the season and buy them in advance, along with cards. Identify gifts you buy in advance by marking the recipient's initials in an unobtrusive corner.

Inventory Control: Supplies, Linens and Laundry

Supplies

Our mothers always had lots of soap, toothpaste, or cleansing powders "laid in." We have, however, lost the knack of stocking up, largely because the storage closets that mother had no longer exist. Consequently, one can be irritated by depletion of such necessities as toilet paper and toothpaste.

The solution is twofold: first, make or find storage space to accommodate one or two months' worth of supplies. Don't feel you must centralize supplies in one single cabinet unless your apartment is very compact. For most dwellings, it is better to devise separate "storage depots" for different materials close to the area where they are used. One depot, in or near the kitchen, will contain backup supplies of dishwashing detergent, cleansing powders, scouring pads, sponges, and probably general housekeeping supplies. Laundry supplies like detergent, bleach, and presoaks will need a place near the washer-dryer. And there should be a bathroom supply area for extra toothpaste, toilet paper, various toiletries, Band-Aids, aspirin, and other sundries.

The "storage depot" space, which won't be used very often—thus making it a #4 in rank—can be somewhat out of the way, but not too difficult to reach. If #4 cabinet or shelf space is already available in the depot area, search no further. If not, consider less obvious possibilities: perhaps an unused shelf or two in a nearby clothes closet, or an extra drawer in a dresser. One client kept the laundry supplies inside an attractive wicker chest used as a coffee table. Another stored bathroom supplies in a cloth laundry bag hung on a closet hook. A box on the floor of the linen closet could be another container. If you are more ambitious, build shelves or a cabinet—perhaps under the bathroom sink.

Once space is set up, buy a two month's supply of toothpaste, soap, mouthwash, deodorant, cleansing powders, toilet paper, and any other regularly used item.

To maintain inventory, hook a permanent pad and pencil to the door or wall of each storage depot. Whenever supplies of any item run low—don't wait until they run out—jot it down on the pad. Collect the various depot slips when you go to the supermarket and bring stocks up to strength. You will never run out of household goods, and this system will encourage you to take advantage of sales and specials.

Linens

If the linen closet is sufficiently generous to hold both sheets and towels, that area is most desirable. If not, keep sheets in the linen closet and store towels elsewhere. If the linen closet itself is insufficient or nonexistent, use the same techniques for finding space that were discussed on page 132 or 221.

Divide the sheets according to type: doublebed flat, twin fitted, and so forth. Choosing characteristic colors or patterns can considerably simplify sorting. For instance, all double-bed bottom sheets could be white, all singlebed bottoms yellow, all singlebed top sheets striped, or whatever pleases you. Some people get proprietary about their "own" sheets, children especially. In that case, provide each bed with a three-week supply of linens that are distinctive enough to identify at a glance.

If towels won't fit in the linen closet, you might be able to keep them right in the bathroom. One client put up a pretty wicker three-shelf rack on the bathroom wall and displayed the folded towels. Another idea is to nail some ordinary plastic buckets to the bathroom door—bottoms affixed to the door—to hold rolled-up towels. Alternatively, keep them in a floor cabinet under the sink, or on a reasonably handy available shelf nearby. Try to keep a three-week supply of towels and washcloths on hand so missing a laundry does not become a catastrophe.

However you store towels, always revolve the towel pile by putting the freshly laundered ones at the bottom. The bottom towels might otherwise mildew or become musty.

Laundry

You can either choose a fixed laundry day during the week, or mark "laundry" on the "To do" list when stocks get low. Neither alternative is inherently more efficient so choose the one with which you feel more comfortable.

Large-family laundry schedules are more complex because, as one client said, "The laundry for my husband, three kids, and me would pile to a literal mountain if I saved it up. I *must* launder at least three or four times a week." In that case, I recommend that each person have his or her own hamper—a basket in bedroom or bathroom would be fine—and launder only one or two hampers at a time. This avoids collecting clothes from each hamper for each wash, sorting each person's things, and redistributing them again—an unnecessary expenditure of time and energy.

Keep several plastic stackable laundry baskets in the laundry room. Sort clothes into the baskets according to the different washing types: whites, colors, permanent press. When each wash-and-dry cycle is completed, sort them back into baskets for folding according to the room or closet in which they belong. Simplify sorting white clothes or children's clothes by putting a colored dot with an indelible marker on the garment where it won't be seen, using a different color for each person.

Apartment-house laundering is slightly different. Try to do the wash in off-hours—very early in the morning or after eight P.M. Stack the dry clothes in the laundry cart according to their placement in the home. If, for instance, the kitchen is near the front door, put the potholders and kitchen towels on top of the laundered pile. Storing then becomes much simpler.

The Task Plan: Sharing the Work

Whether one or both parents work because of financial necessity or personal fulfillment, a side benefit is providing children with an opportunity to make a genuine contribution to the family's well-being. Many children really want to play a role in the family's functioning. Trouble begins, however, when chores seem to be imposed at the parent's whim, as if the child were a servant. The key to effective family cooperation is to assign to each child definite jobs with clear-cut responsibilities and let them work without constant supervision.

Present your proposals in a family council, taking the tack that a well-run household is in everybody's interest. First define the extent to which each child is responsible for his own room and possessions. A toddler of two or three can pick up after himself if the room has been arranged according to his size (see page 230). A four-year-old can lightly dust and make the bed, a child of six can sweep with a small broom, and by the time he is eight or nine he can properly sweep and vacuum. See page 233 for a discussion of how to help the child help himself.

Then list the rest of the tasks—layers 1 through 4—and break down complex tasks into their components. Decide as a group how to delegate and apportion tasks. If family members are consulted they'll feel better about carrying out their tasks. One way to organize the family doings is through the point system. Negotiate a weekly point value for each task based on frequency, length, and difficulty. The point system recommended by Peggy Lennon * works well.

Point Value	Chore
5	Special projects: clean closet, basement, garage
4	Time consuming tasks: vacuuming, cooking a meal
3	Simple tasks: dusting
	Multiply point value by: 3 for daily work
	2 for twice weekly work
	1 for once weekly work

Each person, including parents, contracts for a fixed number of points each week based on ability and fixed time demands. The main homemaker chooses his or her jobs. The rest are distributed among the family according to their point value.

Make it a game if you like by cutting chips out of construction paper. Write the job's weekly point number on one side of the chip and the job on the other. Once a week

*On the Homefront: Speaking for the Management by Peggy Lennon. This is a promotional booklet on home and family management put out by Kentucky Fried Chicken. It's surprisingly useful.

lay the chips out number side up. Each person draws his assigned points without knowing what the jobs are. At week's end, chips are returned to the "chip bowl" for another drawing. To prevent a small child from picking jobs that are too hard put "little people" tasks on different colored chips.

If you don't want to bother with chips, have the family sign up each week for enough jobs to reach their designated point quota. Keep the less desirable jobs rotating. If a child enjoys a particular task let him or her take it over permanently.

However the jobs are allocated, clearly define the time of day when a child's job is to be completed—either before school, directly after school, or by dinnertime. Don't let tasks hang over into the evening.

A Note to Couples

A less complex allocation system can be used for husbands and wives who have trouble delegating the weekly housework load. The key is to view the difficulties that two people experience simply by living together not as an arena for a test of power but as mechanical problems. One of the most common problems is a differing standard of neatness—usually, but not always, the wife is the neater one. One husband, for example, drops his shirts where he stands, according to his spouse. In such a case take note of where he or she generally *does* stand when undressing. Put a "junk chair" (page 149) at that spot so at least all items will be in one place rather than strewn around the room.

If that doesn't work, hammer out a *quid pro quo* deal: you will put his clothes away in exchange for a service— say, washing your car once a week.

Getting husbands to help around the house may also be

a delicate issue. You might discuss which chores are most abhorrent to each of you and try to allocate accordingly. Respect each other's idiosyncracies. One man, for instance, might not mind scraping the dinner dishes but refuses to put them into the dishwasher. Rather than arguing, send him up to get the children ready for bed.

To sum up, whenever a logistical problem between a couple occurs, defuse the irritation by negotiating an arrangement whereby the annoyed party receives some benefit to compensate for whatever aggravation is suffered. Don't dig in your heels on a point of principle.

15
Children

Your child can learn to organize at a very young age. If you simply make it easy for him to take care of himself half your job is done. It is vital, therefore, to arrange and adjust the child's room to his or her needs and capabilities. If the room is well-planned and flexible enough to adapt to the child's changing skills and needs, he will have to go out of his way *not* to keep the room in reasonable order. When the room is ready for the child, you can painlessly teach him the methods of order.

Also discussed in this chapter are the logistics of child care: how to keep track of children's activities and mesh them with your own.

Children's Rooms

First, fit the closet to the child, don't try to fit the child to the closet. Line the closet with plenty of stick-on hooks at the child's eye level. When he can negotiate hangers, insert a tension rod—a metal rod braced with a spring—as a hanging bar. Adjust the bar over the years to the child's increasing height. For a very small child, ages two to four, who might be dismayed by the sheer size of the closet, get a child-sized wardrobe, lined with hooks. Place it, or any new piece of furniture, so as not to disturb your child's movement pattern. One little boy who used an alcove as a "cozy corner" for quiet play before bed became upset when the alcove was blocked by a new wardrobe so it was shifted elsewhere. When the wardrobe is outgrown, switch to the closet.

Check that the clothes you buy have simple catches and fastenings the child can manage himself. Put a small clothes hamper near the closet for the child to put his dirty clothes in as soon he takes them off. Keep the hamper in the bedroom rather than the bathroom; it's too complicated for a child to move his clothes back and forth between the two rooms. Again, he should be able to manipulate the hamper himself.

Choose a low night table broad enough to allow for a lamp, perhaps a small radio, a few favorite books, a doll. Select a dresser low enough so that the child can see over the top. Be sure that the drawers move in and out smoothly without jamming and that the knobs are not too big and shaped so that the child can get a firm grip. When buying furniture, think of the maxim, "Don't give me furniture kids can't walk on." That means durable, maintenance-free materials and fabrics, soft edges, and smooth shapes without fretwork that will catch dust and grit. Bunk beds are especially good space savers for older children who share a room. However, each child should have clearly defined space for himself: hooks with his name on them in bedroom and bathroom, separate closets or wardrobes, a desk (on hinges, to save space), even a curtain or bookcase barricade. This also helps cut down on distraction when doing homework. One frequent question when dealing with kids who share a room is what to do with one child when the other is sick. It's important then, if the illness is more than a matter of spending one night on the couch, to have an alternative arrangement prepared in advance, preferably a convertible couch or daybed that can be made comfortable so the healthy child doesn't feel shunted aside.

Play area—space, pure open space—is very important. If your child is fearless and exploratory open the space up as wide as you can; if he or she tends to stay close to the walls and furniture, enclose the space somewhat as long as it is still wide enough to move around in. Orient the play space toward the corner of the room he tends to gravitate to. Provide enough light to read by and some floor cushions to curl up with. Also try to leave some "secret space" in the room for the child: a bed that's high enough to crawl under or a closet he or she can safely play in.

Select one corner of the play space as a "leave-out" corner where the child is permitted to leave out a jigsaw puzzle or building project in progress. Otherwise all toys should be put away each day.

Many parents naturally think of a single big toy chest for the loose jigsaw puzzle pieces, blocks, torn picture books, crayons, dolls, and all the appurtenances of a twentieth-century child, but that is not the answer. The child gets so frustrated digging to the bottom of the chest to pull something out that he'll fling everything else aside and leave it there until battle lines are drawn. Instead, line the play area with low shelves that create plenty of space for spreading out board games, toys, trucks, erector sets, dolls, and books. The child will have to make a special effort *not* to put toys away. I recommend adjustable shelves that can be raised as the child grows.

Line the shelves with lots of different colored boxes, trays, and jars for loose playthings. It seems to be important to approximately correlate the size of the container with the size of its contents: small boxes for jacks, medium ones for crayons, bigger ones for toy soldiers. This idea comes from a Montessori school attended by the little boy of a friend of mine. She tells me that they shelve the room as I have suggested, and fill the shelves with brightly colored trays of different sizes. The children learn immediately that "the doll goes on the biggish green tray," "the rubber balls belong on the medium red tray," and "the jacks on the small blue tray." Alternatively, just affix bright stickers to cardboard or polyurethane trays. Also, each object should have its own space on the shelf. Kids delight in knowing where things go. There is apparently something in the young child's development that craves clear boundaries and specificity.

A five-point child checklist

Before buying anything for a young child, whether furniture, clothing, or toys, consider the following points:

1. Is it safe? No sharp angles, no small parts that a tiny child could swallow?
2. Can the child manipulate its parts, or learn to do so?
3. Is it on his scale? One two-year-old girl fell in love with a small, dime-store teddy bear, ignoring a larger pretty one. The big one was just out of scale.
4. Can it be adjusted to the child's growth? (Not always applicable.)
5. Is it dirt and stain resistant and/or easily washable?

Teach Your Child to Organize

As soon as your child is able to understand words, introduce one of the basic concepts of organizing: things that are associated with each other are kept together. This is a skill that often has to be taught, ideally between the ages of three and six, when your child is most curious and eager to learn. When he or she is hardly more than a baby, invent categorizing games: distribute a few shoes around the room and let him gather them and bring them to the "shoe place." It is important, even at this early stage, to physically set up the child's room so that he is putting the shoes *away*, not just dropping them in a pile. Use the same idea for clothes and toys.

By the age of three or four the child can grasp the grouping idea more abstractly and can probably be put in charge of his own room. Draw up a five-column chart headed "make bed," "clothes," "underwear," "shoes," "playthings," and cut out appropriate magazine pictures to put next to each heading if your child can't read yet. Leave the categories broad and loose; don't break "playthings" down into "toys," "books," "games," until he is older. Run the days of the week down the side. Duplicate many copies of the chart, which will look like Figure 21.

Each day at a set time keep your child company while he makes the bed and puts everything away. It will be very helpful to provide distinctive trays or boxes for different objects as described on page 232. Your child then works within each category in turn, and you can help out when necessary. Put a gold star in the appropriate box when the category is completed. If your child gets cranky and obstinate, point out the absence of gold stars for that day and leave the rest until tomorrow without recrimination. *Don't* pick up the room yourself either.

When the gold stars became routine for one little girl,

	Make Bed	Clothes	Underwear	Shoes	Playthings
Monday					
Tuesday					
Wednesday					
Thursday					
Friday					
Saturday					
Sunday					

the family was called together for a "Keeper of the Room" graduation ceremony complete with diploma—formal recognition of the child's first step toward responsibility and independence.

Older children, like younger ones, also delight in learning new skills. The problem is that keeping the room neat may already be an issue. Child psychologist Dr. Elaine Blechman* mentions an "elegant solution" which some families have successfully used to avoid problems: the children keep their doors closed and at some point of their choosing during the day, straighten their rooms up, making them available for inspection by a certain time, say 6 P.M. Let the children know specifically what is to be inspected; not only making the bed and straightening up, but more precise jobs—arranging clothes in the closet according to type (see page 144); placing dresser clothes in the right drawer and pile; dividing playthings by type; cleaning jobs like changing sheets, dusting, sweeping, or vacuuming. A chart might be helpful. Make sure, again, that the room is physically set up so that your child can perform these tasks without difficulty. Ask for your child's suggestions about improvements. Encourage mastery by your enthusiastic response and by an occasional reward. When your child occasionally balks, as he will, let the room go until tomorrow but be sure to return to the routine. Your attitude is the most important ingredient. Disorder and confusion are undesirable but not a crime, so moral outrage on your part is inappropriate. Present organizing as you present reading and writing; it is simply a vital skill that must be learned.

Many children become terrific pack rats and simply

*The New York Times, September 2, 1977.

Figure 21 Children's Weekly Chore Chart (*facing page*)

refuse to throw things away so space can become a problem. When the room looks like it's getting out of hand, sit down with your child and gather any objects that haven't been played with for six months or so. Pack them up in boxes for recycling; that is, bring the boxes out again in six months. Many of the toys will have regained their freshness so you won't have to buy as many new ones, and he will probably be less attached to the toys that still seem boring so you can get rid of them.

Adolescents pose a much bigger problem and their chaos is usually the most distressing to parents. A full-blown power struggle may be underway. Are there control problems between you that might be resolved? One teen-age girl, for instance, resented the fact that her mother opened her dresser without permission to put laundry away, and the fact that she had no clear-cut responsibilities around the house but was interrupted from her own activities at whim. She kept her room in chaos as a form of passive resistance. Perhaps helpful physical changes might be made. If neither tactic works, the most practical idea, as long as your teenager fulfills general household responsibilities and limits the chaos to his or her room, is to shut the door and resolutely turn away. Expressing adolescent rebellion through a messy room is a relatively minor problem and will probably be outgrown.

Child Care and Supervision

Maintaining your privacy is vital if you are to maintain your sanity in a family of young children. In addition to the many excellent daycare centers and nursery schools, there are three more informal ways to get the children out of your hair every so often. First, a babysitter, ranging from a doting grandmother to a high school kid down the block. Peggy Lennon* says,

> "When I interview a new babysitter, I always ask these questions to satisfy myself that the children will be safe and feel secure: (1) What would you do if the house caught on fire? If a stranger came to the door and asked to be let in? (determines judgment); (2) What would you do if a child came home crying? (determines warmth); (3) How do you plan to spend time with the children? (commits them to involvement rather than detachment)."

Give the babysitter a list of emergency numbers that includes not only the police, doctor, Poison Control Center, but a relative or close friend to turn to if you can't be reached.

Taking turns sitting with a neighbor or friend is another solution, but the group "sitting pool" is even more flexible and convenient. You agree to sit for other members' children, either in your home or theirs, no fewer than a certain number of hours per month, and you get a certain number of hours from other members.

In a play group, three or four mothers get together and each pledges to care for all the children one morning or afternoon a week. A play group is generally more than simple caretaking; the mother in charge structures the time with planned learning games, crafts, reading, and maybe field trips.

Logistics: School, Activities, Moving Kids Around, and Coordinating

If you have a large, busy family you may find yourself constantly writing permission or absence notes of one kind or

---

* *On the Homefront: Speaking for the Management* by Peggy Lennon.

another. Why not create a "form" note and make copies. Two possibilities are suggested below:

Date_____

Please excuse_____from class on
_____ for the following reason:
_____Rehearsal or performance
_____Medical appointment
_____Other:_____
Thank you.

Signed: _____
Hope McClain

Date_____

_____ has my permission to engage in the following activity:
Thank you.

Signed: _____
Hope McClain

Sort and handle the memos *from* school, scouts, church, as you would any other paperwork (chapter 5, page 65), but try to do it every day so nothing gets past you.

To generally keep track and control all family activities get a *big* monthly calendar with the *biggest* date squares you can find. Hang it where everyone will see it, probably in the kitchen. At the beginning of each month, fill in all the kids' regular appointments—ballet lessons, swimming lessons, Cub Scout meetings—on the calendar. As each child tells you of special events—a birthday party, costume assembly, a Brownie cookout—mark it on your personal calendar or have the child write it in. Note on your personal calendar whatever preparatory plans have to be made and on the appropriate day enter them on the To do list. Using the calendar as your guide, make chauffeuring and pickup arrangements as far in advance as you can. Work out long-term cooperative arrangements when feasible. If you live in the city, older children can often take young ones along to school or other activities.

Appendix

Furniture manufacturers

Bunting Company
1771 Tomlinson Road
Philadelphia, Pennsylvania 19116

Burris Industries, Inc.
Domani Division
Burris Boulevard
Lincolnton, North Carolina 28092

Charlton Company, Inc.
111 Crawford Street
Leominster, Massachusetts 01453

Drexel Heritage Furnishings Division
Drexel, North Carolina 28619

Dunning Industries, Inc.
6001 West Market Street
Greensboro, North Carolina 27409

Murphy Door Bed Company, Inc.
40 East 34th Street
New York, New York 10016

Raymor Moreddi
% Raymor/Richards, Morganthau Co.
734 Grand Avenue
Ridgefield, New Jersey 07657

Bibliography

The books marked with an asterisk are those I consulted during the writing of this book. The others will be interesting reading if you care to pursue those topics.

Time

* BLISS, EDWIN C. *Getting Things Done: The ABC's of Time Management*. New York: Scribner's, 1976.

* LAKEIN, ALAN. *How to Get Control of Your Time and Your Life*. New York: McKay, 1973. (Paperback: New American Library, Signet edition, 1974.)

MACKENZIE, R. ALEC. *The Time Trap*. New York: AMACOM, 1972. (Paperback: McGraw-Hill, 1975.)

LUCE, GAY GAER. *Body Time*. New York: Bantam (paperback), 1973.

Money

PORISS, M. *How to Live Cheap but Good: A Primer for People with High Tastes and Low Income*. New York: McGraw-Hill (Paperback).

Decorating and the Uses of Space

CONRAN, TERENCE. *The House Book.* New York: Crown, 1976.

* KATZ, MARJORIE P. *Instant-Effect Decorating.* New York: M. Evans, 1972. (Paperback: New American Library, Signet edition, 1973.) A very direct, common-sense approach to decorating and utilization of space.

* LIMAN, ELLEN. *The Spacemaker Book.* New York: Viking, 1977. (Paperback: Pocket Books, 1978.)

* LIMAN, ELLEN and PANTER, CAROL. *Decorating Your Room: A Do-it-Yourself Guide.* New York: Franklin Watts, 1974. Although purportedly written as a primer for children, many grown-ups will find this basic information useful too.

SKURKA, NORMA. *The New York Times Book of Interior Design and Decoration.* New York: Quadrangle, 1976.

* STODDARD, ALEXANDRA. *Style for Living: How to Make Where You Live You.* Garden City, N.Y.: Doubleday, 1974. Stoddard's approach to decorating is very similar to my approach to organizing. Find out what pleases you most and work around it.

If you plan to do your own work, these "handyperson's how-to's" will be useful:

Better Homes & Gardens Handyman's Book. New York: Bantam (Paperback), 1974.

CURRY, BARBARA. *Okay, I'll Do It Myself: A Handy Woman's Primer.* New York: Random House (Paperback), 1971.

Reader's Digest Complete Do-It-Yourself Manual. New York: W. W. Norton, 1973.

Home and Family Management

BERMAN, ELEANOR. *The Cooperating Family: How Your Children Can Help Manage the Household—For Their Good as Well as Yours.* Englewood Cliffs, N.J.: Prentice-Hall, 1977.

* BRACKEN, PEG. *I Hate to Housekeep Book.* New York: Harcourt, Brace & World, 1962. (Paperback: Fawcett Crest, 1965.)

KALTMAN, MARY. *Keeping Up with Keeping House: A Practical Guide for the Harried Housewife.* Garden City, N.Y.: Doubleday, 1971.

* EISEN, CAROL G. *Nobody Said You Had to Eat Off the Floor* . . . . *The Psychiatrist's Wife's Guide to Housekeeping.* New York: McKay, 1971.

* LENNON, PEGGY. *On the Homefront: Speaking for the Management.* Published by Kentucky Fried Chicken, 1976. Can be ordered from Daniel J. Edelman, Inc., 221 North La Salle Street, Chicago, Illinois 60601, free of charge.

* SKELSEY, ALICE. *The Working Mother's Guide to Her Home, Her Family and Herself.* New York: Random House, 1970.

URIS, AUREN. *Executive Housekeeping: The Business of Managing Your Home.* New York: Morrow, 1976.

Kitchen

BEARD, JAMES et al. (Eds.) *The Cook's Catalogue.* New York: Harper & Row, 1975. A compendium of kitchen gadgets and devices.

CONRAN, TERENCE. *The Kitchen Book.* New York: Crown, 1977.

* U.S. DEPARTMENT OF HOUSING AND URBAN DEVELOPMENT. *Designing Kitchens for Safety.* (Pamphlet). Order from U.S. Government Printing Office, Washington, D.C. 20402. Stock #2300-00266.

Other

BATTERBERRY, MICHAEL & ARIANE. *The Bloomingdale's Book of Entertaining.* New York: Random House, 1976.

* KOBERG, DON and BAGNALL, JIM. *The Universal Traveler: A Soft-Systems Guide to Creativity, Problem-Solving and the Process of Reaching Goals.* Los Altos, Calif.: William Kaufmann, 1974. (Distributed by Crown). Organizing difficulties are often linked to problems with general decision-making. This book offers some useful insights into the process.

Index